944/05

NAPOLEON

WHO WAS...

NAPOLEON

The little general who wanted to rule the world

ADRIAN HADLAND

Illustrations by Alex Fox

✳ SHORT BOOKS

First published in 2005 by
Short Books
15 Highbury Terrace
London N5 1UP

This edition 10 9 8 7 6 5 4 3 2 1

A CIP catalogue record for this book
is available from the British Library.

ISBN 1-904977-10-3

Printed in Great Britain by
Bookmarque Ltd, Croydon, Surrey

For my son, Nicholas

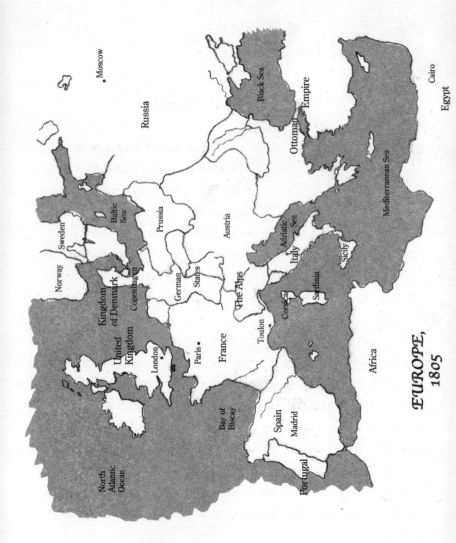

EUROPE, 1805

North Atlantic Ocean

Norway

Sweden

Moscow

Russia

United Kingdom

London

Paris

France

Kingdom of Denmark

Copenhagen

Baltic Sea

Prussia

German States

Austria

The Alps

Bay of Biscay

Spain

Madrid

Portugal

Toulon

Corsica

Sardinia

Italy

Adriatic Sea

Sicily

Africa

Mediterranean Sea

Ottoman Empire

Black Sea

Egypt

Cairo

CHAPTER 1 – INVASION!

Boulogne, French coast, 1805: He stood like a statue on the high, white cliff, gazing intently through a spyglass at the horizon. At last the day had come. Any minute now, the wind would shift and a line of sails would appear on the horizon. The French fleet! What a glorious moment it would be. Finally, after eight years of planning, Napoleon Bonaparte, Emperor of France, would cross this ditch called the Channel and take what was rightfully his: England.

Only the other day he had promised Josephine, the Empress: "I will take you to London, Madame. I intend the wife of the modern Caesar to be crowned in Westminster Abbey." Yes, wouldn't that be grand? Once England was won, the rest of the globe would soon follow. His armies would conquer the world. He would build the biggest empire in human history: greater than Augustus Caesar's, greater than Charlemagne's, reaching further even than the lands ruled by Alexander the Great himself.

Napoleon moved the spyglass round and looked at the green coast of Kent. It seemed so close. He could see the houses with smoke rising out of their chimneys. He could see people chopping wood and doing the washing. He could even see children playing in the garden. As he looked, he chewed on a piece of liquorice. Napoleon loved liquorice and always kept a good supply in his pocket. He kept it in a fancy tortoiseshell box. He wondered whether they sold good liquorice in England. He might just have to take some with him. Napoleon was good at that sort of thing: at planning what to take on a trip. The trip he had in mind was more than a picnic, though. He was planning an invasion. He wanted to invade England.

You need a lot of stuff for an invasion. First you need thousands and thousands of soldiers, the more the better. Then you need to train them properly. If you don't, they will just get beaten in the first battle and what's the point of that? Then you need to make sure the soldiers have uniforms and guns and plenty to eat. Hungry, cold soldiers with no guns are not going to win any battles. So you have to build factories to sew uniforms, and armouries to make guns, and bakeries to bake bread. Quite a few of the soldiers will need horses too, so you better take lots of them. And you might also think of taking some doctors because some soldiers are bound to be injured or get sick. And then when you have got all these soldiers and horses and doctors and food and guns together, you have to find enough boats to put them on. And you don't just need one or two boats. You need thousands of them. You need fishing boats and row boats and sail boats and gun boats. You need all the boats you can get your hands on from every port. And then you need to build more because you probably don't have enough.

This was what Napoleon had been doing for eight years: finding the soldiers, training them, building factories and bakeries and building ships to carry his army to England. It had been quite a business, but Napoleon loved planning big things like battles and invasions. He loved it so much he threw in lots of extras. He even asked a songwriter to come up with a good invasion song. As the soldiers arrived in England, they would all sing the song together. He also had the idea of putting all the really short men together and getting them to practise holding on to the tails of horses. This meant that when they arrived in England, these short men could hang on tightly and travel at the same speed as the soldiers riding the horses. Brilliant!

But Napoleon had a problem. It was a rather big problem. He had the soldiers, the food, the guns, the weapons, the boats, the song, the horses and even the short men. What he didn't have was an empty sea to sail across. The Channel was not just 25 miles of choppy water, after all. It was filled with the ships of England's Royal Navy. And these weren't just ordinary ships. These were the best, fastest ships in the world. They had loads of guns. They had the best sailors. They even had the best admiral of all, Horatio Nelson.

Napoleon dropped his spyglass down from the Kentish coast, over the sea and found the ships of the Royal Navy. He chewed his liquorice faster and faster. Just beyond the harbour wall, the British ships sailed back and forth. The English ships were like sharks waiting for Napoleon to go for a swim. They sailed so close, he could hear them shouting from the deck. "Come on, Boney! Come for a swim!" That's what the English called him: Boney. English mothers told their children that if they were naughty,

Boney would get them. Sometimes he was called "the Corsican ogre" because he was from an island called Corsica and because they thought he was a monster.

But Napoleon had a trick up his sleeve. He always did. That's why he won so many battles. This time, his trick was this: he would get a few French ships to sail past the Royal Navy and go as quickly as they could towards the far-off islands of the West Indies. Admiral Nelson and the English would then sail after them. The French ships would then secretly turn around and sail back again. On the way they would meet up with lots more ships from Spain. Then the French and their Spanish friends would all arrive back in the Channel at the same time, while Admiral Nelson and the English were still thousands of miles away in the West Indies. Napoleon would then put all his men on their boats, and sail across undisturbed to England. The trip would only take about eight hours, so by the time Nelson got back, it would be much too late. The French soldiers would then jump off their boats, singing their invasion song, and march to London. They would beat the English army in a battle. And then, Napoleon and Josephine would become the King and Queen of England. Simple!

But where were the French and Spanish ships? Where was his fleet? And where on earth was his Admiral, Pierre Villeneuve? Napoleon had been waiting and waiting. Two weeks ago he had written a letter to Admiral Villeneuve:

"Sail," he had said. "Do not lose a moment, and, with my squadrons reunited, enter the Channel. England is ours. We are ready…" But still there was no sign. He had never liked that Admiral Villeneuve, but there was nobody else. All the best French admirals had either left the navy or they were dead. Admiral Villeneuve, with his puffy white wig, his chubby chin and his endless excuses, was all Napoleon had.

Eventually, Napoleon gave up. He put away his spyglass and turned back. He walked along the sandy footpath leading off the cliffs and down to the dunes below. Though only five foot two, he was a well-built man with a high forehead and broad shoulders. He stuck out his chest when he walked. He was wearing his favourite uniform, that of a colonel of the guard. It was a simple uniform considering he was an Emperor: white and black with red cuffs and gold epaulettes. As usual, he tucked his right hand into the white waistcoat as he walked and his famous long grey overcoat billowed out behind him.

His officers knew from his face that there was still no sign of Admiral Villeneuve. The little general was even paler than usual as he made for the small, run-down house where he was staying. The house was on a hill. Napoleon had chosen it because it overlooked the very beach from where Caesar himself had set out to invade the British Isles hundreds and hundreds of years ago. How Napoleon wished he could do the same.

But who was this Napoleon? Did he really think he could invade England and then rule the world? How was it that a young boy from the distant island of Corsica grew up to become the Emperor of France and one of the greatest generals since Caesar, Alexander and Charlemagne? For the answers to these questions, and to complete the story of the invasion of England, we need to go back to the beginning, back to a very small island in the Mediterranean, in the year 1769.

CHAPTER 2 – REBEL CHILD

Corsica, 1769: All across the small Mediterranean island of Corsica, the bells were ringing. Since the first light of dawn their cheerful clangs had sounded out over sleepy villages and towns. Families stirred from their slumber and rubbed their eyes. Then they smiled. They remembered that today was a holiday. August the 15th was an important religious festival in Corsica. To show it was special, colourful flags were draped from house windows. Fresh, green twigs and branches were stuck to doors and walls. The churches were filled with flowers.

Villagers and townsfolk spent the morning preparing for the big service at the cathedral in the town of Ajaccio. They washed their faces, brushed their hair and put on their best clothes. Outside, the summer heat grew fiercer by the hour. By noon, the island shimmered like a hot oven. As the excited islanders made their way to the cathedral that day, many noticed the young, heavily pregnant woman who walked among them, slowly but proudly. "There goes Letizia," they said. "What a brave woman."

Her name was Letizia Bonaparte. Everyone knew the story of how she and her husband, Carlo, had fought the French soldiers during the Corsican war for independence. Corsica had been sold to France by a country called Genoa just two years earlier. None of the Corsicans wanted to be French; nor had they wanted to remain part of Genoa. They just wanted to be Corsicans. Carlo and Letizia had joined the fight for freedom against the French. They had hidden and fought in the mountains for almost a year; they had ambushed French columns, blown up supply wagons and taken pot shots at French soldiers. Carlo, Letizia and the small band of fighters had been constantly on the run from the French soldiers. They'd eaten berries, wild animals and whatever they could find. Their clothes were in shreds, their boots worn through and they had sheltered from the freezing winter storms in caves.

The people of Ajaccio knew the story of how one day, 19-year-old Letizia, six months pregnant and nearing the end of her strength, had lost her footing crossing a mountain torrent. She was within a moment of being swept away before a hand reached out and grabbed her. How different history might have turned out if she had fallen that day. But Letizia, Carlo and baby Joseph all survived. When the war was over, they returned to Ajaccio.

They were a young family and had very little money. But slowly, they began to rebuild their lives. Carlo landed a decent job as a court assistant. And before long they moved into quite a fancy home by Corsican standards. It had three storeys, a flat roof and shutters on the windows. It was painted bright yellow, though the colour quickly faded in the harsh Mediterranean sun. The Bonapartes lived on the ground floor.

As she walked to the cathedral on that festival day, Letizia could feel the people pointing and staring. She didn't mind, though. She was proud of her fight against the French. She was also proud of her big tummy and the child inside her. She wondered whether it would be a boy or a girl. Letizia was a striking-looking woman with a narrow face, a big nose and wide eyes. She had long, dark, wavy hair. She hated to waste money and spent very little of it on herself. Her husband Carlo was quite different. He liked to order the latest fashions from Paris. He wore the smartest clothes and spent more money than they could afford. They were quite a couple, opposites in many ways. She was a simple, modest person; he an extravagant dreamer.

Almost as soon as the villagers and townsfolk had settled into the packed cathedral and the service had begun, Letizia began to feel sharp pains in her stomach. And then, she started having her baby. Luckily, the Bonapartes lived only a few minutes walk from the church. She managed to get home, with some help from her friends and family, but there was no time to get her to the bedroom. Instead, Letizia gave birth to a little boy on the sofa. The baby had an intelligent face, screamed loudly and was soon happily sucking his thumb. In Corsican folklore, thumbsucking so quickly was a very good sign. At birth, though, the baby had not been well, so he was quickly baptized. He was named Napoleon after an uncle who had recently died and also because of a favourite Egyptian martyr, Neapolus.

When Joseph was seven years old and Napoleon was six, another son, Lucien, was born. Elsa followed two years later, then Louis, Pauline, Caroline and, finally, Jerome. Eight children in all! It wasn't long before Napoleon began to boss them all around. He was a tough little chap with piercing grey eyes and a shrill voice. He had a horrible temper and thought nothing of bullying his brothers and sisters and getting his own way. His nickname at home was Rabulioni ("The Disturber"), because he liked to make trouble. He was especially interested in mechanical things and annoyed all the adults by asking them question after question about how things worked. He wanted to know this; he wanted to know that. How did the water mill work? How did ships sail? The questions were endless.

Occasionally, Napoleon was a little naughty too. One day he stole some figs from a tree in the garden. It was a special tree and he was expressly forbidden from touching it. But the figs were so sweet and juicy he couldn't help himself. Just as he was tucking into the lovely fruit, the gardener spotted him.

"What do you think you are doing?" asked the gardener.

"I am eating these figs," replied Napoleon.

"If your mother catches you she will thrash your backside."

"You will also be in trouble," said Napoleon. "You are meant to be looking after the trees."

"You are right," the gardener said, thoughtfully. "Well you had better run along. And don't take any more."

Napoleon was pleased with himself. He had eaten some lovely figs and got away with it.

The next morning, Letizia happened to pass the tree. She noticed immediately. Someone had stolen her figs. She called the gardener and demanded to know what had happened. When Letizia Bonaparte was angry, she was very angry indeed. The gardener soon owned up and Napoleon was in big trouble, not for the first time. Letizia believed strict discipline was the only way to handle children. In those days, that meant children were hit over and over again with a belt or hand when they did something wrong. After stealing the figs, Napoleon got a very sore bottom indeed.

From his youngest days, like many boys, Napoleon wanted to be a soldier. He had a toy drum and a wooden sword. He was good at drawing but only liked to draw soldiers. He made friends with the real soldiers in Ajaccio and exchanged his own white bread for their coarse, brown bread military rations. He loved to walk to the docks to listen to Corsican sailors tell stories about the battles they had been in. Sometimes he was taken out to sea in one of the fishing boats. One evening he stayed outside in a terrible thunderstorm, getting soaked from top to toe.

"Where have you been?" asked his mother when a sodden Napoleon walked in.

"I have been standing out in the rain," replied Napoleon.

"What on earth for?" asked Letizia.

"Because when I am a soldier, I will be ready for any weather," said Napoleon.

When he was a little bigger, one of Napoleon's favourite things was to ride on horseback on his own through the countryside. He loved smelling the sweet bush called maquis that you find in Corsica, as well as the oranges and lemons growing in the groves. He thought Corsica must be the most beautiful place in the world. The tips of the granite mountains were always covered in snow. On their upper reaches were pines, firs and evergreen oaks. Lower down, chestnut trees clustered on the slopes. In the valleys and on the plains, mulberry bushes and olive trees gave shade to sheep, goats, foxes and pigs. Napoleon loved to watch the waves crashing on to Corsica's rocky shore. He also enjoyed chatting with the people who lived up in the mountains. Everyone was amazed at how interested the little boy was in everything. They also noticed that sometimes he liked just to sit quietly, thinking. He seemed to be angry but he never uttered a word. They wondered what he was thinking about that could make him brood so darkly.

Carlo and Letizia knew that one day Napoleon would make a good soldier. They agreed they should send him to a special military academy, if they could. In fact, they thought he should try to be a sailor with all his experience on sailing boats. But there was no such place to train soldiers or sailors on Corsica. So, at only nine years old, Napoleon was sent to a far away military boarding school in France.

As Carlo and Letizia didn't have much money, they applied for a special scholarship from the King of France. This was hard to do as Letizia and Carlo hated the

French: only a few years before they had almost given their lives fighting against them. Still, they wanted the best for Napoleon. The family was very pleased and excited when Napoleon was granted the award.

In April 1779, little Napoleon packed his bag and, accompanied by his father and by his brother Joseph, made the journey from Ajaccio to the mainland of France by boat and then by road to the distant province of Champagne, north east of Paris. There, in a small town called Brienne, was the military school. The family had decided that Joseph would be a priest. So after the two brothers said goodbye, Carlo took Joseph to the church school to begin his training for the priesthood and left Napoleon to start his future as a soldier.

Napoleon was very unhappy at the Brienne military school. The other boys made fun of his strange, Corsican accent and they thought his name was hilarious. They laughed at his threadbare clothes. They mocked him for working so hard. They bullied him. They gave him the nickname "The Spartan" after the ancient nation of warriors from Sparta who had thrived on discipline, simple food and tough living conditions. As a King's scholar, Napoleon had very little pocket money. He wrote to his father saying that if he couldn't have more pocket money, he wanted to leave the school. Carlo didn't reply.

During the five years he spent at Brienne, Napoleon grew very thin. As he was training to be a sailor, he slept in a hammock. He was given only a single blanket, even in winter. He tried to work hard to impress his teachers but they didn't seem to notice his efforts. Secretly they all noticed how determined he was but they were all very harsh when he made mistakes. Punishment was always severe at the academy.

One very cold day, the boys decided to fight a war in the courtyard. Napoleon had an idea about how they should build a fort out of snow and was soon directing the building. Before long, a full-scale fight was under way. Stones with snow packed around them were used as the cannon balls of the artillery. The little boy with the strange accent seemed to grow a little that day, as he pointed to his classmates where to attack, called them back in defence and helped build the fort that protected them. Already he was showing the makings of a future general.

Napoleon was very good at maths and he loved reading about the great figures from the past, like the Roman emperor Caesar and the Greek hero Ulysses. His school report said he was tough, proud and stubborn. Ideas always seemed to be bubbling in his head. But he never looked like he was very well. His skin had a yellow tinge. He had very thin lips and few friends. He missed his family terribly, especially his older brother Joseph.

During the course of 1784, it became obvious that even though Napoleon would be graduating from Brienne, he was not going to make it into the navy. Only a small group of pupils were selected for naval careers, and they were chosen mainly on the basis of the wealth and position of their families. Carlo was bitterly disappointed, but he was determined to do the best he could for his son. He wrote a letter to the war ministry asking that Napoleon be allowed to enter the most famous military school in France, the Ecole Militaire in Paris. The ministry agreed, on condition that Napoleon first passed an examination. He did, with flying colours. In a report on the young Corsican, his examiners noted his "commanding character". Napoleon was in.

In late October, 15-year-old Napoleon and four other Brienne graduates arrived in Paris to finish off their education at the famous Ecole Militaire. The school was housed in a very imposing building right in the centre of the city, just off the capital's Champ de Mars (Field of War). If they could survive a year at the Ecole and win the coveted graduation sword, an excellent military career was sure to await them. Napoleon was one of 120 "gentlemen cadets" at the school, all between the ages of 13 and 15. On arrival, he was shown to his very small room and introduced to Alexander des Mazis, his roommate. Alexander was a little older than Napoleon and the two were soon the best of friends.

Napoleon and Alexander were fitted with a smart winter uniform. It had a blue jacket lined in red and topped with yellow. In May, they would switch to their summer uniforms, which were just as elegant. Like all the other boys, Napoleon was issued with a dozen shirts, collars, handkerchiefs and socks. All the boys ate together in the main hall with 30 boys at each table. After the wholesome but dull fare at Brienne, the food at the Ecole was fantastic: five-course meals with all the trimmings. But Napoleon didn't really enjoy food or eating and he found the huge plates of meat and all the puddings a bit disgusting.

Some of the boys at the Ecole Militaire even brought servants with them, who brushed their uniforms and polished their shoes. They also had grooms to look after their horses. This appalled Napoleon who wondered how these cadets could possibly make good soldiers if everything was done for them by servants. Napoleon thought that living in luxury hardly prepared these young men for the tough conditions of a real war.

Alexander and Napoleon worked hard during that year and helped each other along. Alexander noticed how Napoleon often walked on his own, his head lowered, not noticing anything else going on around him. Sometimes he smiled and gestured while he walked and talked to himself. When they were relaxing, Napoleon often spoke of Corsica and of how he wanted, one day, to go home. He imagined himself to be the liberator of Corsica who would go home to set the island free.

In the boys' last few months at the Ecole Militaire, Napoleon was told that his father had collapsed and died. Carlo had suffered for several years with severe stomach pains. It was stomach cancer, in the end, that killed him. If Napoleon was sad, he didn't really show it. Usually, boys who suffered tragic loss were taken to the school infirmary for a chat with the priest. Napoleon said he didn't want to do that. After writing a long letter to his mother expressing his sorrow, he got back to his work.

It wasn't long before the hard year at the Ecole was over. Napoleon and Alexander tried as best they could. While they both came nearer the bottom than the top of the class (Napoleon came 42nd out of 58 cadets and Alexander came 56th), they both graduated. They were presented with the long, shining, cherished swords that marked them as graduates of the famous Ecole Militaire. And then, as luck would have it, both of them were assigned to the same regiment: the well-known artillery regiment called La Fère, based in the town of Valence. With their swords at their sides, the two friends set off to begin their new lives and make their fortunes.

CHAPTER 3 – REVOLUTION

In the spring of 1789, Napoleon was ordered to gather his things and prepare to march. He hurriedly put his things in his pack, grabbed his gun and rushed to join his unit. But he would not be shooting a cannon or taking part in any big battles on this trip.

"Soldiers," the officer in charge shouted. "Members of the public are rioting. We have been ordered to march to the town of Seurre to put an end to the trouble."

With that, the small detachment of soldiers, including Napoleon, marched out of the barracks and down the road toward Seurre. This was quite exciting for Napoleon. Only once before had he seen "action" with the regiment. That was when the silkworkers in Lyons had gone on strike a few months before. By the time Napoleon had got there, though, the strike was over. Even the three ringleaders had already been hanged. Perhaps this time they would get there on time?

As they marched, Napoleon wondered why the people of Seurre were so unhappy. He had heard from the other soldiers that there was trouble brewing in Paris, too. He had even heard people whisper about a revolution, whatever that was. He reminded himself to find out about this thing called a revolution. What could it mean?

As the small group of soldiers marched into the town of Seurre, Napoleon realized they had missed everything once more. The riot was over. A number of buildings were burning, but the angry crowd had gone. The streets were empty. Napoleon and his unit were ordered to remain in the town for several weeks in case there was more trouble. While they waited, Napoleon thought he would ask around to see what had happened. It seemed the trouble had been about the King, Louis XVI.

"The King's run out of money," said a shopkeeper. "So he wants us to give him more. Fat chance."

From the people of Seurre and articles in the newspapers, Napoleon figured out what was going on. The King had apparently called all the members of his Parliament to meet at Versailles Palace just outside Paris. It was the first time in more than 150 years that Parliament, which was called the Estates General of France, had been called together. Previously, the King hadn't thought he needed the Parliament. But now the King was desperate. He needed money.

Rather than give the King more money, however, the estates general decided it was time to change the whole system of government in France. The King had to go, they decided. It was time the French people had more of a say. The Revolution, which really just means big change, had begun.

The Revolution didn't mean much to Napoleon; not at first, anyway. The La Fère regiment stayed in its barracks and didn't get involved. Even when things turned really ugly, the army kept to itself. But slowly, Napoleon began to notice changes. For one thing, the names of the months were changed. Napoleon and most of his friends found this a bit confusing. The new government decided that the year the King was thrown off his throne and a new republic was established, 1789, was to be known as Year One. And just to make sure everything changed, each month was given a new name. In this way, Thermidor roughly corresponded with August, Brumaire with November and Vendemiaire with October.

Then Napoleon noticed that many of the regiment's senior officers were leaving. The old King had had his head cut off. The rich nobles were said to be next for the chop. And, as most of the officers were nobles, they feared for their lives. So they joined a huge number of people, 150,000 or so, who left France. They were known as the émigrés, and vowed only to come back when a new King was back on the throne.

It was strange not having many of the old senior officers around, Napoleon thought to himself. But the good bit was this gave everyone else a chance to move up through the ranks. Napoleon was made a captain of the artillery. This would not have happened in the old army. Before the Revolution, only the rich nobles had risen quickly through the ranks or become senior officers. Now everyone was getting a chance. Napoleon was beginning to like the Revolution. He read all he could about it. The more he read and the more he saw, the more he liked it. He soon became a strong supporter of the new regime, and was even fined for talking too much about it in the officer's mess.

In the meantime, he got on as best he could with his training. The artillery school at Valence was one of the best in France. Napoleon loved it. He learned all the skills needed to shoot various kinds of guns: advanced maths, the workings of cannon, howitzers and mortars, the manufacture and storage of gunpowder, laying sieges, map-making and map-reading. He spent three days a week in class and three days a week in the field practising on different guns.

After work, he relaxed in a bookshop where he was allowed to rent books. Sometimes, he saved enough from his small wage packet to buy a book or two. He buried himself in reading about history and politics. Every now and then, he read right through the night.

But, while he enjoyed the training, Napoleon was very homesick. He wasn't eating well and he was working very hard. His pay was very meagre and he could barely afford a single meal a day. His younger brother Louis came to stay and Napoleon had to feed Louis and pay for his schooling. Napoleon got so sad and lonely at times he even thought about killing himself. But he knew that, with his father gone and so many brothers and sisters to support, his family was relying on him.

The hard training was eased a bit when he met pretty Caroline de Colombier. Napoleon fell head over heels in love with Caroline. She was his first love, and he hers. They used to go for early morning walks up in the hills. They munched on cherries and laughed together. These were precious moments, but Napoleon was determined not to let anything interfere with his training.

During these first few years, Napoleon continued to read everything he could get his hands on. He read all he could about the military campaigns of the great generals Alexander, Hannibal and Caesar. He read everything from the history of the West Indies to philosophy and the natural sciences. His friend Alexander used to tease him about all the work. "Why should you care what happened a thousand years ago?" he asked Napoleon. Napoleon didn't really have an answer. He just enjoyed reading and hoped that perhaps one day all this knowledge would come in useful. Alexander wasn't interested in reading. He was much more interested in parties. He couldn't understand why Napoleon kept reading about the past. While Alexander stayed out all night, Napoleon was in bed by 10pm and was up at 4am to work. It was as if he was preparing himself: for what, he didn't know.

Napoleon visited home in Corsica on quite a few occasions while he was learning the art of artillery. Indeed, he got into serious trouble for his long absences from the regiment. At times, he risked being thrown out of the army altogether. During his many trips to Corsica, he became heavily involved in local politics on the island. He even tried to encourage a revolution there, just like the one in France. Eventually, because of this, Napoleon was kicked out of Corsica and his family was forced to leave the beautiful island. Letizia took Napoleon's younger brothers and sisters to live in France. They had very little money and they travelled from village to village looking for somewhere to live.

Just as things got tricky in Corsica, they got nasty in France. The new government had started chopping the heads off anyone who was against them. They had devised a new killing machine called the guillotine, which has a sharp, angled blade that hangs off a scaffold. The victim is tied below the blade with his or her neck under where the blade falls. When the lever is pulled, the blade drops from the top of the scaffold and slices the victim's head off. Hundreds and hundreds of people were killed in this way. Napoleon thought it was horrible. He kept quiet, though. Anyone who complained too loudly risked losing their head.

By early 1793, Napoleon was terribly down. He didn't know where his life was headed. He was barred from his beloved Corsica. His family was homeless. His new country, France, was in a complete mess. His army career was in ruins. He had applied to join the Army of the Rhine because he knew that at least that army was fighting some real battles. But his application was refused. Then, in July of 1793, opportunity came knocking for Napoleon. He was about to start climbing the ladder to fame and fortune.

CHAPTER 4 – NAPOLEON'S
FIRST BIG BATTLE

Toulon, September, 1793: General Jean Carteaux was a fine-looking man with a sweeping black moustache. He was one of the flashiest generals around and always inspected his troops in a bright scarlet and gold uniform. General Carteaux was also famous as a painter. His battle-scene paintings and his portraits of people were especially good. As a military leader, however, he was close to useless. He didn't have any experience at all in a real battle. The only reason he was a general was because the army didn't have many generals. Most of them had left when the King lost his throne.

For two months, General Carteaux and his people's army had been trying to get into the town of Toulon. Toulon was one of several big towns in the south of France that wanted the King back. The townsfolk had pulled down the red, white and blue flag of the French Republic and raised the white fleur-de-lys emblem of the Bourbon monarchy. Usually with a siege, if you waited long enough, the defenders would run out of food or ammunition, or both. But at Toulon, this wasn't going to happen. This was because in the middle of the siege, English and Spanish ships had sailed right into the Toulon's large, well-protected harbour to lend a hand to the royalist defenders. The ships brought food, ammunition and soldiers from England, Spain, Naples and from Piedmont. Together they easily kept General Carteaux at bay.

To make matters worse, the officer in charge of General Carteaux's artillery, Captain Dommartin, was so badly wounded he was sent home. The problem was that nobody other than Captain Dommartin knew how to work the cannon properly. "Where the heck am I going to find an artillery expert?" General Carteaux asked himself.

Just then, in to the army camp rode Napoleon Bonaparte, artillery captain. Admittedly, Captain Bonaparte was long-haired and dressed shabbily, but at least he knew something about guns. Napoleon had come to the camp to visit an old friend. He could see General Carteaux's army was in a mess. For a start, there were only a few cannon. There also wasn't much ammunition and few of the tools needed to make the cannon work. But at least General Carteaux was fighting a real battle. When General Carteaux offered Napoleon command of his artillery, Napoleon accepted immediately. Because he was known to have a bit of a temper, General Carteaux soon gave Napoleon the nickname of Captain Cannon.

"Ah, Captain Cannon, good morning," shouted the general on seeing Napoleon arrive for his first day of work. "I was just going to inspect our gun battery at Montaubon. Perhaps you would like to join us?".

"Certainly. That would be an honour, General," Napoleon replied.

They rode about a mile before arriving at the battery. Its guns were pointed at Toulon. "So what do you intend to do?" the General asked the gunnery sergeant by the cannon. "We will build an oven, general, so we can heat up the cannonballs until they are red hot," he said. "Then we will fire the cannonballs at the enemy's ships and set fire to them."

"Excellent plan. What do you think, Captain Cannon?" the General said, turning to Napoleon.

"I think, General, we should test how far the cannons fire before building the ovens," replied Napoleon.

"Very well. Test fire the cannon," General Carteaux ordered the sergeant.

A cannonball was found and the cannon was loaded with the ball and some gunpowder.

"Fire," shouted the gunnery sergeant.

Boom, went the cannon.

The general, Napoleon and the gunnery sergeant watched as the cannonball soared up into the sky, faltered, and then fell to earth. It hadn't reached even a third of the way to the walls of Toulon.

"It must be the gunpowder, General," said the sergeant. "Those damn Royalists must have sabotaged it."

Napoleon shook his head. He knew the cannonball would get nowhere near the ships. It had nothing to do with gunpowder. The guns were simply too far away. Napoleon knew he was going to have to come up with a very clever plan if he was going to help Carteaux's army get the better of the royalists holed up in Toulon.

The following morning, Napoleon rode to the highest hilltop to look out over Toulon and plan what he was to do. He had visited the town of Toulon many times. The bay and sea beyond reminded him of his home in Ajaccio. Standing now on a hill called Le Six Fours he scanned the landscape through his spyglass. Before him was Toulon, its high walls bristling with the guns and cannons of its defenders. Napoleon's lips tightened when he saw the English flag flying over the port together with the white fleur-de-lys.

"Damned English," he muttered to himself. "Always interfering where they are not wanted."

He looked closely at the town and its fortifications. Toulon was an old port built around the fourth century. It was now a very secure naval base. Facing south, Toulon nestled at the foot of Mount Faron. The slopes of the mountain formed a semicircle around the town walls. The defenders placed forts on the high ground that made any attack by land very difficult.

In the distance Napoleon could see the Mediterranean coast. The sea flowed into Toulon's vast outer harbour and then was pinched through a bottleneck of land into a much smaller harbour. The enemy ships were all moored safely in the inner harbour. Suddenly, the answer to his vexing puzzle came to Napoleon. In an instant, he realized how he could outwit the royalists and the English and all the others defending Toulon. The point where the land pushed in to make the bottleneck was only protected by a small fort. If he could capture this fort, Fort Mulgrave, he could shoot his cannon at all the ships in the inner harbour. The ships would be then be forced to leave, taking their foreign troops with them. It would only be a matter of time until Toulon ran out of food and ammunition. Fort Mulgrave was the key. If he took it, Toulon would fall. But it would take some weeks to put all the pieces of his plan into place.

As head of the artillery, Napoleon's first task was to get the artillery working. He rode to nearby army supply depots, wrote letters, dispatched orders, begged and pleaded. Within a few weeks, he had gathered more than 100 long-range mortars, 24 cannon and enough ammunition, equipment and gunners to make use of them. Now he was getting somewhere. He never left the guns. He slept on the ground wrapped in his cloak, even when the autumn rain turned the ground to mud. Some said he looked like a ghost as he had dark rings under his eyes and his skin was tinged yellow. Meanwhile, General Carteaux was so pleased with Napoleon's progress in building up the artillery ready for battle, he promoted him to Battalion Chief.

Now the real test came. Napoleon presented his plan to General Carteaux. It consisted of a pretend frontal attack on one side of Toulon to distract the defenders. This would draw many of the defenders to one side of the town. Then, while the defenders weren't looking, he would launch an all-out assault on Fort Mulgrave, the small outpost that protected the entrance to the harbour. Napoleon would use all the artillery he had gathered to support the attack on Fort Mulgrave. Then, once the attack succeeded, he would bombard the ships in the harbour with red hot cannonballs so they would either set sail, surrender or be sunk. It was a brilliant plan. Even General Carteaux agreed. At least it would keep the hot-headed Captain Cannon quiet, he thought to himself. He promoted Napoleon to Adjutant-General.

But General Carteaux's heart wasn't really in the fight. He was only a painter, after all. Instead of putting into practice Napoleon's plan, he ordered a few weak attacks of his own that failed. Napoleon grew frustrated. It now became clear to all that General Carteaux was the problem. Before long, he was replaced with a new general. This time, a proper attack was planned with Napoleon at its head. Instead of directing the guns, he led the charge at the head of an infantry battalion.

The real assault began one cold, miserable day in the middle of December. Pouring rain turned the ground to mush and a freezing wind scoured the battlefield.

"We can't fight in this," said the new general. "We shall have to try again on another day."

"We must go on," insisted Napoleon. "If the weather is bad for us, it's just as bad for them. They won't be expecting us to attack them in this weather. We must continue."

The general looked him in the eye, then gazed out at the storm. "Very well, Adjutant-General Bonaparte. We will do it your way."

As flashes of lightning and rumbles of thunder shook the sky over Toulon, the French attack began. Napoleon rode at the front, urging his men through the driving rain. Just then, his horse collapsed. It had been shot. Napoleon picked himself up from the mud, then ran on toward Fort Mulgrave.

"Come on," he shouted. "Come on." Napoleon ran at the English soldiers with his sword at the ready. He slashed and hacked as he ran. One English soldier stabbed Napoleon in the calf with his bayonet. Napoleon shrugged off the wound and stumbled on. The French soldiers saw for themselves the determination and bravery of the man dubbed Captain Cannon.

In what seemed like a few minutes, Fort Mulgrave was taken. The defenders gave up or were dead. Now it was time to reclaim the harbour. The cannon at the fort were carefully turned around and pointed at the ships in the harbour. This time Napoleon knew the cannons would reach them. Cannonballs were warmed up so they were red hot, then loaded into the cannon.

"Fire," shouted Napoleon. The redhot cannonballs blasted into the dark, stormy sky. They rained down on the ships in large, fiery arcs. Two of the ships in the harbour were storage ships filled with gunpowder. When they were hit by Napoleon's redhot cannonballs, they caught fire and then exploded.

All of Toulon heard the explosions. The sky filled with flames. Some of the ships made it out of the harbour, carrying with them as many foreign soldiers and supporters of the French King as they could. The rest of the ships were caught by the cannonballs. Thirteen of them burned like huge bonfires before sinking beneath the waves. The defenders gave up. Toulon had fallen, just as Napoleon had said it would.

Napoleon was a hero. Everyone knew it was his plan that had led to the fall of Toulon. At the age of 23, he was promoted to Brigadier-General. His pay was increased from 1,000 francs a month, which wasn't very good, to 15,000 francs, which wasn't bad at all. He was given a new job: Inspector of Coastal Defences. He was given a small château in the pleasant seaside town of Antibes. He quickly arranged for his mother and his brothers and sisters to vacate the horrible place they were living in. From a slum in the town of Marseille, they moved in to a warm and sunny home.

The spring and summer of 1794 were happy times for the Bonapartes. At last, their star was rising. The dark, bad days had all but gone. The future was filled with hope. A better life beckoned. Letizia was delighted at the family's change in prospects. As usual she tempered her joy with a no-nonsense dose of reality. "Just so long as it lasts," she always used to say, "just so long as it lasts".

At this point Napoleon's brother Joseph decided not to join the priesthood and became a soldier like his brother. This made Napoleon very angry. He didn't think Joseph would make a good soldier. He thought he should be a priest. Joseph went ahead anyway, joined the army and took a job in the supply depot. He also married Julie

Clary, the daughter of a local businessman. And what Napoleon could not deny was that Julie's younger sister, Desirée, aged only 14, was rather attractive. Yes, he definitely fancied her.

Napoleon and Desirée started dating. After a few months, they decided they loved each other and wanted to get married. Napoleon braced himself to ask Mr Clary's permission.

"Mr Clary," Napoleon stuttered.

"Yes, Napoleon, what can I do for you?".

"I would like to ask your permission for Desirée's hand".

"Desirée?"

"Yes, Mr Clary. We love each other very much. I would like to marry her".

"That is impossible," replied Mr Clary.

"Impossible?" said Napoleon.

"Julie is already married to a Bonaparte. I will not let Desirée marry a Bonaparte too. One Bonaparte in the family is enough. You may not marry Desirée."

Napoleon was heartbroken. Desirée was in tears. But Mr Clary's mind was made up. There would be no wedding. Napoleon swore he would always care and look out for Desirée. Time would show that he kept his promise.

But the good times didn't last long, as Letizia feared. In those days, people's fortunes changed as quickly as French politics. Those who were heroes one day, had their heads cut off the next. There were many people who were jealous of Napoleon's rapid rise to fame. In July 1794 the leaders of the government who had promoted Napoleon were sent to the guillotine themselves. Suddenly most of the powerful people who liked Napoleon were gone. The new government wasn't so sure about him. Maybe he wasn't on their side at all? Maybe he was a Royalist who wanted the King back? Napoleon was thrown in prison while they decided what to do with him.

Luckily, Napoleon still had a few important friends. They persuaded the new government that the little general did not want the kings brought back to France. So, after two weeks of fearing he might be sent to the guillotine, Napoleon was released from prison. His family was greatly relieved. But things were a long way from the glorious days after Toulon.

In early May of 1795, Napoleon broke the seal and unwrapped a letter from army headquarters. They were his new orders. They would tell him which army he would be joining. When he read the words, he couldn't believe it. He had been told to report to the Army of the West. Disaster! The Army of the West was the worst possible job he could have imagined. The army was fighting against Royalists within France. This was not the sort of war Napoleon was interested in. He wanted big battles against foreign countries. He didn't want to run around arresting people like a policeman. He was a soldier, a brigadier-general in the artillery. He could not accept the posting. He decided to go to Paris to see what he could do to have the order changed. By another stroke of fortune, Napoleon made for the French capital at exactly the moment his skills would be called upon once more.

CHAPTER 5 – SAVING THE DAY

Paris, 1795: Napoleon set off for army headquarters early as usual. Perhaps today he would hear some good news? As he didn't have an army, he wasn't being paid. He had sold his carriage to pay his hotel bill and he had precious little money left. But he still had a good horse. He climbed up into the saddle and trotted off toward the heart of Paris.

It was a marvellous, summer day. He was 26-years-old and the hurly-burly of the big city excited him. His mouth dropped open as he watched elegant ladies ride past in their fine carriages. He enjoyed riding through the city's beautiful parks and gardens. They were filled with strong-smelling flowers and exotic trees.

He rode past a fair and strained to see. The fairs in Paris were always brimming with new things he had never seen before. He'd seen a man at one who could swallow a whole sword and a Spaniard at another who could drink boiling oil. Paris was full of strange-looking people from distant lands. Wealthy couples strolled arm-

in-arm along the broad, elm-lined boulevards. They nodded at Napoleon as he trotted by.

Posters on the wall announced free exhibitions and
lectures on science and the arts. He thought he might
go to one or two, especially as they were free. He smiled
at the pavement silhouette artists who cut the shape of
people's faces from paper. In seconds they cut with scis-
sors the faces of beautiful women in hats or handsome
men with twirly moustaches.

When he rode past the Palais Royale, he tried not
to look. In the shadows among the billiard salons and
cafes, women dressed in what looked like their underwear
whistled and called to him, as they did to all the men who
rode by.

As a Brigadier-General, Napoleon now had a small
staff to assist him with his duties. He had chosen two
men who had impressed him during the Toulon siege,
captain Auguste Marmont and sergeant Andoche Junot.
Napoleon's younger brother Louis also joined him. But
Napoleon felt bad for his three companions. His refusal
to join the Army of the West meant he wasn't being
paid. The little money he had had run out quickly. It was
then that life became very hard for the four young men.
They hardly ate. Their clothes were more frayed by
the day. They had been waiting for months while
Napoleon tried to get his orders changed. While they
waited, they shared a room in one of the cheapest,

dingiest of hotels in the seedy Latin Quarter of Paris.

But Napoleon was having no luck at all in getting out of joining the Army of the West. Army headquarters had refused to give him a new job. The general in charge had been an artillery officer for 40 years and had never fought in a battle. He was jealous of Napoleon's success and thought a stint fighting Royalist rebels would prove Napoleon's loyalty – and take him down a peg or two. He sent Napoleon a letter saying he had been struck off the roll of active duty generals for refusing to report to his post. Napoleon knew he just had to hang on a little while longer. Something would come up. Fortunately for him, he was right.

One late October afternoon, Napoleon was out doing some chores in the city when he heard the news that a Royalist army was gathering in Paris. They wanted to rid France of the Republican government once and for all and put the French kings back on the throne. People said the Royalist army was a big one. Troops and volunteers and members of the national guard were coming from all over to join it. Someone said they reckoned there were 25,000 soldiers in the Royalist army and it was growing all the time. That was far more than the government had to protect itself. But Napoleon knew there was always a way to outwit an army – no matter how much bigger it was than your own. "Perhaps the government could use me," Napoleon thought to himself.

He carefully made his way through the frightened crowds to the palace, called the Tuileries. Here, the government was growing more and more nervous. The president was a man called Paul Barras, who looked more worried by the minute. Messengers brought him news:

"The Royalist army is led by General Danican, Citizen President."

"The Royalist army has 25,000 soldiers."

"The Royalist army will march on the palace first thing tomorrow, Citizen President."

"The Royalist army will split into two columns of 12,000 men and march on the palace from different directions."

"Only a few have come to help us, Citizen President."

With each piece of news, President Barras' face turned more and more grim. He rubbed the back of his neck. Perhaps he would feel the guillotine's blade on it tomorrow. His messengers ran across the city calling for help. Hardly anyone came. He had only 5,000 men ready to defend the palace. They were outnumbered five to one. Would this be the end of the French Revolution? Would the Bourbon kings soon be back in charge?

In the midst of this worrying, in walked Napoleon. He wasn't much to look at. He was barely five foot tall, skinny, with tatty clothes and long, lank hair. He could see the defenders were rushing here and there but didn't really know what they were doing. He was a Brigadier-General of the artillery and he had an idea that he thought might help. He introduced himself to President Barras.

"Citizen President, I am Brigadier-General Bonaparte. If I may suggest, I think we need cannon if we are to defend ourselves," he said.

"Thank you for coming, Brigadier-General. But I am afraid we don't have cannon," the President replied.

"But I know where you can find some," said Napoleon, with a smile and a twinkle in his eye. "Not far from here, in the suburb of Neuilly, is the Sablons artillery park. There you will find plenty of cannon. If you put them in the right place, you will have the better of General Danican tomorrow".

"Well then we must fly," said the President. "Major Murat!"

A dashing cavalry officer came bounding up. "Yes, Citizen President."

"Go to Sablons," said President Barras. "Take a troop of your men. Bring back as many cannon as you can carry."

"Yes, Citizen President."

"And Major Murat."

"Yes, Citizen President?"

"Ride like the wind."

With that, Major Murat turned on his heel and ran to fetch his horse and men.

Time was running out. General Danican's troops were

busy preparing. They would attack the next morning. They polished their muskets and sharpened their swords. The streets were full of men at arms. One rumour said General Danican was already on his way to fetch the cannons at Sablons. Murat had to move quickly. Every minute was precious. He gathered a troop of his cavalry together and galloped out of the palace. The horses' hooves clattered on the paving stones. France's fate rested on their mission. Already General Danican's troops were close by, and Murat and his men had to hack at Royalist soldiers with their swords to get free.

In the palace, Napoleon, President Barras and the 5,000 defenders waited nervously for news. Hours went by. The sky darkened as evening came. A storm brewed over the city. Suddenly, there was the sound of hooves and shouting at the gates. "Murat is back!" a voice said. "He has the cannon!" Napoleon moved swiftly into action. He knew General Danican's troops would advance on the palace along two key roads. Here he placed his cannons and waited.

As the famous day known as the 13th of Vendemiaire dawned, the rain came. It thundered on to Parisian roofs and gushed down muddy streets. General Danican waited, hoping the weather would clear. He didn't want to attack in the rain. He sent dozens of messengers out with instructions: do this, do that, don't forget the other. His troops sheltered from the downpour as best they could.

As they waited, the morning turned to midday. Still the rain came down. In the Tuileries Palace, a dark cloud of gloom settled over the defenders. But the few extra hours gave them time to check their equipment, make sure the gunpowder was kept dry and point the cannon in the right direction. Then all they could do was wait.

In the middle of the afternoon, General Danican at last gave the order to advance. Two columns, each of more than 10,000 soldiers, marched up the main street toward the palace. Because there were regular soldiers, volunteers and onlookers all crowding the street, the advance became disorganized. Orders were shouted, but in the excitement no one listened. The crowd marched quicker and quicker. Soon the advance became a charge.

Napoleon stood by a line of his cannon at the gates of the palace on a wide street called the Rue St Honoré. His heart was pounding. He faced out on to a square and watched as the Royalist army poured down the street ahead of him and charged toward the palace. They looked more like a rabble than an army. Napoleon stood waiting, his men at the ready. He was drenched. He lifted his arm and could feel the water run down the sleeve of his sodden blue coat. His lifted arm was a signal to the gunners to take aim. They did so. When General Danican's forces were only yards away, Napoleon's arm fell. His cannons roared. The entire front of the approaching column collapsed in a terrible heap of blood, bodies and burned uniforms. The same happened to the second column of people, its front torn out by Napoleon's cannons.

As the shock set in, and General Danican's soldiers stood stunned and horrified, Napoleon waved Murat's cavalry into action. The sight of hundreds of horsemen, swords raised at full gallop, sent the attackers into panic-stricken retreat. The battle was soon over.

Napoleon had saved the government. General Danican's men were killed, captured or chased into the countryside. Once the city was safe, Napoleon returned to the palace. He was cheered by the president and by the ministers. Once more, he was a hero.

Napoleon was the talk of Paris. He was instantly promoted to the rank of full general. He was made second in charge of the Army of the Interior. He was given a grand mansion, a splendid carriage and a team of staff officers, servants and clerks. His hefty new pay package allowed him to entertain new friends at lavish lunches. He was seen at the most exclusive parties. Even though he didn't like dancing, he appeared at the best balls. All eyes were on the small figure and youthful face of Napoleon that summer, including those of a charming woman by the name of Josephine de Beauharnais.

CHAPTER 6 – THE SEDUCTRESS

What was it about Josephine? Certainly, she was beautiful. She had long, chestnut hair, a small, slightly turned-up nose and lively, sparkling eyes. She was graceful too. She had long limbs, elegant fingers and she moved liked a dancer. And she had an amazing voice: soft, clear but with an enchanting Caribbean lilt. But the way she looked, the way she moved, the way she sounded doesn't explain what it was about Josephine that made her irresistible to most men who met her. For one thing, she had black, rotten teeth. This was because she spent too much time gnawing sugar cane on the plantation in the West Indies where she grew up. She tried not to show her teeth and put her hand in front of her mouth when she laughed.

In spite of her ugly teeth, men simply could not resist Josephine. They fell over themselves to be with her. They spent fortunes buying her gifts and presents. They left their wives and girlfriends to spend time with her. She was like a flame surrounded by fluttering moths. Soon, one of those moths was General Napoleon Bonaparte.

One day, Napoleon was sitting in his fancy new office in Paris. He was a full general now and enjoying all the trappings of his success: the smart carriage, the new uniform, the small army of staffers, the big, comfortable office with a view. There was a knock at the door.

"Yes, come in," said Napoleon. It was one of Napoleon's officers.

"General, there is a small boy here to see you," said the officer.

"What does he want?" asked Napoleon.

"He has come to ask for his father's sword."

Napoleon looked annoyed. He had ordered every person in Paris to surrender their weapons. Still, if it was just a boy, perhaps he would at least hear him out.

"Oh very well, send him in," said Napoleon.

The young man walked in to the office and stood before Napoleon.

"Good day, General," he said. "My name is Eugène de Beauharnais. Thank you for seeing me."

Napoleon looked the young man up and down from behind his desk. He was a well-dressed, handsome lad. "How old are you Eugène?" asked Napoleon.

"I am 14 years old, General."

"And what is it that I can do for you, Eugène?"

"My father was the Viscount Alexandre de Beauharnais. They cut his head off at the guillotine."

Napoleon could see there was great sadness in the boy's eyes but also lots of courage.

"I am sorry to hear that," said Napoleon.

"My mother and I and my sister Hortense have no one in the world. We would like his sword to be returned to us. It was precious to him and would be a comfort to us."

"You know I have ordered that all swords and weapons are to be handed in," said Napoleon. "I can't have people running around causing trouble with them."

"Yes, General, I understand. Only my mother and I don't plan on making any trouble. We would just like his sword back."

Napoleon stood up from his desk and walked over to Eugène. He reached out and grabbed the lobe of his ear and squeezed. This was a sign of Napoleon's tender affection.

"Oh, very well, Eugène," he said fondly. "You have spoken well. Your father's sword will be returned to you and your mother."

A smile came over Eugène's face. "Thank you, general."

A short while later, there was another knock at the door.

"It is the boy's mother, Josephine de Beauharnais," said the officer.

Napoleon rolled his eyes back and sighed. Whatever

next, he thought. He had so much to do. Still, he may as well get it over with.

The door to his office opened once more and this time, Josephine walked in. Napoleon was immediately smitten.

"I am Josephine de Beauharnais, mother of the boy you treated so kindly this morning. I came to thank you, personally, General. You have done us a great favour," she said.

"Your boy did you proud," stammered Napoleon. "Your accent is unusual, where are you from, madame?"

"I was born in Martinique. But your accent is unusual too, general. Where are you from?"

"I too am from a small island. My home was Corsica."

"Two islanders, cast adrift in the big city," said Josephine, looking into Napoleon's grey eyes. They both laughed, Josephine with a hand across her face to hide her teeth.

"I would like to see more of you, madame," said Napoleon.

"Then you must come and visit me in my salon," replied Josephine.

And with that, she was gone. Napoleon looked at the space where she had been standing for some time. A big smile crept onto his face and stayed there, on and off, for the rest of the day.

As Josephine was helped aboard her carriage in the yard below, a curtain flickered high above in a window. A dark figure was watching from the shadows.

"So, my little dove, you have met the General," the figure said to himself. "Good." President Barras was pleased. The plan was working, so far. There had never been any doubt that Napoleon would be bowled over by Josephine. Now, it was only a matter of time. Then at last she would be off his hands. No more fortunes on dresses. No more jewels or cashmere shawls. No more presents, money or gold. Perhaps he would visit her salon from time to time. But the cost of keeping Josephine would be over. A younger man would take over now. That younger man was General Bonaparte, the toast of the town. But Josephine always pushed a hard bargain.

"He must be the head of an army. How else will he be able to afford me?" she had demanded from President Barras.

"Very well," he replied. "But which army?"

"And you can't leave Napoleon in Paris or how will we see each other? You must make him the head of any army somewhere else."

"Yes, my dove," said President Barras. "Then you will marry him?"

"If he asks me, yes," said Josephine.

"Oh, he will ask you all right," said Barras. "He will most definitely ask you."

President Barras then began to think of where he might send Josephine's future husband. Napoleon had made it clear he preferred the big battles to the basic policing done by the Army of the Interior. Barras remembered that Napoleon had refused to take up his post at the Army of the West, which had brought him to Paris in the first place. "How about the Army of Italy?" President Barras thought to himself. He smiled.

Based in far-off Nice, the Army of Italy was in utter shambles. It consisted of a large group of some 30,000 hungry, unpaid, poorly equipped and very dispirited officers and men. It was said that their uniforms were so tatty that some of the officers wore goatskins to keep warm. When the soldiers' shoes fell to pieces, they wrapped woollen coverings round their feet. They stole these from the local peasants. For two years, the Army of Italy tried to stay out of trouble and out of the harsh, Alpine weather. In the snow and blizzards, the last thing they felt like doing was marching off to fight. Even if they did, the chances were they would bump in to the dreaded Barkets. The Barkets were groups of criminals and deserters who killed anyone they came across and stole their money and clothes.

In charge of such an army, Napoleon could hardly do any harm. In any case, Italy was so crowded with armies from other countries, it was called the battleground of Europe. Armies from Austria, Piedmont, Sardinia, Spain, England and France jostled with the Barkets. Dividing things further, the Pope controlled several states in central and northern Italy. The Army of Italy was exactly like the country: chaotic and divided. It was just the right way to keep Napoleon occupied – and paying Josephine's bills. Perfect. The Army of Italy it was.

Napoleon, of course, fell helplessly under Josephine's spell. He was a 32-year-old general with Paris at his feet. Like all the other men who Josephine charmed, he was deeply in love. Napoleon proposed marriage to Josephine and was pleased and excited when she said "yes". The word had hardly passed her lips, when President Barras announced Napoleon's promotion to Head of the Army of Italy. He would be leaving Paris two days after the wedding to take up his position.

Letizia, Napoleon's mother, however, was very much against the wedding. She disapproved of Josephine. For one thing, Josephine was 36 years old. This was much too old to be a bride. It was probably too old to have children. Letizia had heard the stories about Josephine. She knew Josephine lived a loose and scandalous life. There were many stories about how she danced naked for her men friends and took part in debauched parties. Some of the most important men in France visited her in her salon. There was even a story that she had no money at all and was terribly in debt. Some said she lived off presents and gifts from her lovers. That made her virtually a prostitute, in Letizia's eyes anyway. No matter that she had no other way of surviving after the death of her husband.

But Napoleon was as stubborn and determined as always. He wanted to marry Josephine and he went right ahead and married her. Letizia (or Madame Mère, as Napoleon and his brothers and sisters called their mother) was not amused.

And so it was that at 8 o'clock on the evening of the 9th of March, 1796, Josephine, President Barras, a couple of friends and the registrar, waited patiently for Napoleon to arrive at his wedding ceremony. Madame Mère chose not to attend. Since his posting to the Army of Italy, Napoleon had been very busy. He was working on a plan.

As seemed to be common on days of importance for Napoleon, the weather was awful. The rain came down in sheets. "I hope he hasn't forgotten," Josephine murmured, the clock showing it was well past 8 o'clock.

"He's extremely busy," replied President Barras. "He's making his last preparations for Italy."

Josephine didn't respond. She only gazed into the crackling log fire. Perhaps she was thinking of the old lady fortune-teller back in Martinique who had told her: "One day you will marry a superman and mount a throne." Well, if he was a superman, he was a late one.

Just before 10 o'clock, the door flew open. In charged Napoleon. "Wake up, sir," he shouted at the registrar, who had drifted off to sleep. "Marry us, quick!"

The registrar jumped up and staggered over to the

marriage register. He began to fill out the marriage certificate.

"Age?" he asked Josephine.

"32," she replied, demurely taking four years off her real age.

"Age?" the registrar asked Napoleon.

"33," he said, politely adding one year to his.

Soon, the certificate was signed and read out and Napoleon and Josephine were declared man and wife. The married couple left immediately.

"Thank you everyone," Napoleon shouted as they climbed aboard their carriage.

The marriage didn't get off to a good start. On their wedding night, Josephine's little pug dog, Fortune, bit Napoleon on the leg in a fit of jealousy. Two days later, a carriage drew up to Josephine's house. The honeymoon was over. Napoleon climbed in and headed for Italy to take command of his first real army.

CHAPTER 7 – NAPOLEON'S
FIRST REAL ARMY

The Italian Alps, March, 1796: Napoleon sat on his horse, peering through the mist. It was just before dawn and very cold. There was hardly a breath of wind. He pulled his cloak tighter around him and watched the warm air from his lungs turn to an icy cloud as he exhaled.

He knew that a few hundred yards ahead lay the centre of the Austrian army. They were probably asleep. Napoleon chuckled to himself: What a surprise they would get when the mist lifted. He looked to his left, then to his right and grunted in satisfaction. His soldiers, the French Army of Italy, were ready. During the night they had marched quickly and quietly to this place just outside the town of Montenotte in the Italian Alps. Now everything was in place. Their cannon were loaded and pointed at the Austrians. The infantry had fixed their bayonets to their muskets and stood quietly in formation. The horses of his cavalry pawed the frozen ground with their hooves. Thousands of French soldiers waited for Napoleon to give the word to advance.

But Napoleon waited. He wanted the sun to melt away the mountain mist before he gave the signal to attack. He wanted to see the look on the Austrian generals' faces as they wiped the sleep from their eyes, and saw row upon row of French bayonets glinting in the early morning sunlight.

It was close to a miracle that the French Army of Italy was actually about to fight a battle. A few months ago they had been a bunch of hungry, cold, tired men who hadn't fought or been paid for months. Now they were a keen, fit army ready for battle. How had Napoleon done it? The way he always did things: by working hard, by taking care of every detail and by coming up with a brilliant plan.

Napoleon smiled to himself as he remembered arriving in the town of Nice to take charge of this army. His generals had thought him a complete idiot. True, he was only 32 years old and he had never been in charge of a real army. But he'd never been given a proper chance. He would soon show them, he had told himself. Now, even his generals were impressed. In those first few weeks Napoleon had rushed around trying to organise things. No one had ever seen a general with so much energy. He issued hundreds of detailed orders. He paced up and down in his office, his right hand tucked into his waistcoat, speaking as quickly as he could. Two secretaries took turns in writing down everything he said. Then it was put neatly in a letter ready for Napoleon to sign. Once signed, the letters and orders were carried off to be delivered. All day couriers came and went, carrying off Napoleon's letters and bringing back the replies. In this way Napoleon issued lots of orders.

Pacing up and down, rattling off orders and letters, Napoleon began to mould the rabble into an army. He paid his troops for the first time in months by twisting the arms of some local bankers to lend him the money. He made sure his soldiers were given decent food. He ordered new uniforms and boots. He removed a few troublemakers. He replaced old muskets and brought in fresh, new troops. He rounded up extra horses and mules. He got rid of suppliers who were stealing from the army and fined villages for failing to provide what they promised.

When he wasn't dictating letters or orders, Napoleon was out on his horse checking on his army. He praised his men when he saw good things and punished them when he saw bad things. He spent whole days on his horse, riding from regiment to regiment, gathering information, sleeping by campfires. He had huge maps drawn up with details of the number and location of his soldiers as well as those of the enemy. Nobody could read maps better than Napoleon. Some said he read them like a musician reads music. He employed a geographer to draw huge scale maps and the two men stretched full out on the floor to scrutinize every detail. Sometimes they got so excited they bumped heads.

Poring over his maps, Napoleon had come up with a brilliant plan. So far, it had worked perfectly. That was why his army was now lined up in the mist ready to attack. That was also why the Austrian army had no idea what was about to happen. Napoleon had known, even before he arrived to take charge of the French Army of Italy in the spring of 1796, that he would be facing two main enemies, the Sardinians and the Austrians. Together, these two armies were much bigger than Napoleon's army. However, he figured out that if he could somehow separate the Austrians from the Sardinians and keep them apart, he could fight them each of them on their own. This meant he would fight two small armies instead of one big one. He much preferred those odds!

Napoleon's plan went like this: he pretended to march his army towards the town of Genoa where the Sardinian army was encamped. When the Sardinians heard that Napoleon was approaching, they thought Christmas had arrived early. They were so sure they could beat Napoleon, they marched out of Genoa and went as fast as they could up the coast to meet him. But instead of fighting the Sardinians, Napoleon left only a few troops to defend a town in their path called Voltri. He then sent the rest of his army on a secret night-march away from the coast and the Sardinians and through the Alps. On the other side of the mountains, the Austrian army was relaxing. They thought they were safe. They thought Napoleon was about to fight the Sardinians. They were wrong.

Napoleon rubbed his hands in glee. The Austrians didn't have a clue what was about to happen. They had camped in small groups in a long line through the mountains. They thought they were protected by the deep ravines and high slopes of the Alps. But their safety was also the thing that threatened them most. For it would take hours, possibly even days, for the whole Austrian army to gather in the same place. Napoleon would concentrate his entire French force at the centre of the Austrian line and, when the sun came up, he would crush it. After that, taking care of the Sardinians would be easy.

Napoleon could feel the sun on his face. He closed his eyes as the bright light reflected off the white, snow-capped mountains. The mist was lifting quickly. Every now and then he caught a faint glimpse of the Austrian lines. Soon there would be total panic. He lifted his gloved hand ready to signal the attack. A flurry of anticipation surged through this troops. The moment had come. The battle was about to begin.

"Artillery, begin firing!" ordered Napoleon, dropping his hand. Suddenly the silence of the Alps was replaced by the great booming of the little general's guns. Napoleon first real battle at the head of a real army had begun.

Many miles away, on the other side of the mountains, the Sardinians looked up and listened. As the sound of Napoleon's distant cannon echoed over the high ridges, the Sardinians realised they had been tricked.

There was no French army before them in the town of Voltri. The Sardinians had been deceived into leaving Genoa and into abandoning their friends, the Austrians. Now they must rush back and hope they were not too late. But they were indeed too late. Napoleon caught the Austrian army by surprise and smashed it. Then he beat the Sardinians too.

Montenotte was only the first move on Napoleon's chessboard, however. His bigger plan was to kick all the other armies out of Italy altogether. And it all went like clockwork. Time and again his columns surprised the enemy. At the battles of Arcola and Rivoli, the French moved quicker and fought harder than expected. They seldom took on bigger opponents head on. If he was forced to, Napoleon made sure he did so in a narrow space where he could put his best, toughest veterans in the front rank. More often, Napoleon first divided the enemy army, then forced a wedge between the two bits to ensure they couldn't get back together again. Then Napoleon beat the two smaller armies, one by one. He beat the Piedmontese and he beat the Austrians. Even his most unwilling generals saw that Napoleon's way meant victories. An army that had sat around doing nothing for two years was now breaking through the Alps and into the heartland of northern Italy. Cities and towns fell before them: Parma, Piacenza, Modena, Bologna, Pavia, Milan and Venice.

Wherever they went, Napoleon's armies seized the spoils of their victories. Most of the good stuff, the priceless artworks and statues, the cash, gold, silver and even the best horses were shipped back to Paris. There they were received by a very grateful government that had almost run out of money. The Pope, desperate to save the Italian Church's treasures, actually paid Napoleon millions in diamonds to leave him in peace.

News of Napoleon's victories spurred celebrations in Paris. After years of being beaten, suddenly the French army was victorious. Its divisions, like a swarm of locusts devouring a cornfield, consumed, destroyed or stole almost everything they could lay their hands on.

On the 10th of March, 1798, Napoleon told his army: "You have won victory in 70 actions and 14 pitched battles; you have taken more than 100,000 prisoners, 500 field pieces, 2000 heavy guns... 30 million francs for the treasury and 300 masterpieces of ancient and modern Italy which it needed 30 centuries to produce."

In battle after epic battle, Napoleon rid Italy of all who challenged him. With each victory, his reputation grew. Napoleon – the saviour of the Revolution and defender of the Republic! There were times when Napoleon came within an inch of his life. He insisted on riding at the front of his army where he could see and hear everything that happened. Sometimes, he got too close. During the battle of Arcola, the French army had got stuck fighting for a bridge. Napoleon had to capture the bridge and use it for his troops. So he stood up and personally led his soldiers across, fighting with his sword as he went. But, just as the bridge was almost won, Napoleon slipped. He fell down the bank and into the swampy water. On his own he would certainly have drowned. But his younger brother, Louis, Captain Marmont and two soldiers linked arms and pulled him out.

With each victory, his soldiers loved Napoleon more. He always treated them well. He handed out gifts, promotions, titles and money to those who had performed well in battle. He paid for the education of children who had lost fathers and he restored some pride in France's achievements and nationhood. When Napoleon asked his soldiers to march as fast as they could, they ran. When they marched up and down for days, unclear where they were going, they knew the little general had a plan. Always, the enemy was taken aback at the speed of the French army.

"We don't march, we fly!" the French soldiers boasted.

After 12 major battles in 18 months, the Austrian army

finally gave up, signed the Treaty of Campo Formio and retreated to Vienna. Napoleon had conquered Italy. When the news reached Paris, the city erupted with joy. Posters were tacked to every wall reading: "Italy is taken!"

People poured out of houses, shops and workrooms. They spread over the squares and danced in circles holding hands. They lit big bonfires and cheered. Workmen crossed the Seine River by boat to join the festivities on the site of the old Bastille. This was where Parisians celebrated victory, and now Napoleon had conquered Italy. What a party they had that night.

CHAPTER 8 – UNDER THE EYE
OF THE SPHINX

Sahara Desert, 1798. "Water," the soldier whispered. "Water."

His mouth tasted like ash. His tongue was swollen and furry. He could think of nothing other than fresh, sparkling, gushing water. He hadn't drunk anything for days. Then, he looked up. There it was, the water he had dreamed of: lots of it. A whole lake full of water. With his last energy, he climbed to his feet. He started to run.

"Water," he shouted. "Water!" His fellow soldiers saw it too. They also started to run.

"Water!" they shouted. They dropped their guns. They threw off their packs. They ran and ran. They could almost taste it, feel it.

But the water never got any closer. The harder the soldiers ran, the more the water stayed out of reach. They ran until they could run no more, then collapsed. They died believing there was water just a few steps further. Napoleon watched from his horse, and shook his head.

"That vision of water is a terrible thing," he told Captain Marmont. "How can it look as if there is water just over there and when you get there, it disappears?"

"I don't know, general, but many of the men are falling for it. They are dying running to the water, when there is none."

"Remind me to look into this strange phenomenon when I get to Cairo, captain".

"Yes, general. More watermelon?"

Napoleon and his men didn't have much water but they did find some watermelon strangely growing in the desert. If you sucked the flesh, it was almost as good as a glass of water. Watermelon saved their lives. But there just wasn't enough to go round.

They had been marching through this hellish desert for almost two months. It had been two months of agony. They had run out of water and had little food left. The hot sun pounded down on their tired, sunburned bodies. If anyone was left behind or wandered off on their own, they were killed by angry Arabs.

"Can't be much further now," said Napoleon. He felt bad about the suffering he had imposed on his men. But he knew it would be worth it. Soon they would be in Cairo. Soon they would see the palaces and churches of the old city. They would see the pyramids and smell the perfumes of the east. They would eat their fill of dates and dishes flavoured with exotic spices. They would gather enough gold and treasure to fill a thousand wagons and return to France as conquering heroes.

After his success in Italy, things had got too quiet for Napoleon in France. The Austrians had been beaten. So too had the Sardinians and the Piedmontese. Italy was now part of France. Napoleon thought a new adventure was just what was needed. He would like to have invaded England. Indeed Napoleon wanted desperately to defeat the English. He was tired of the English Royal Navy ruling the waves. He was fed up with the English giving money to the Austrians and the Prussians to attack France and he was especially irritated with the English for plotting time and again to kill him.

But his ships and soldiers weren't ready yet. So how about conquering somewhere else first? He had always fancied the east. Perhaps it was because he was named after an Egyptian martyr, perhaps he just liked how old and mysterious everything was. The pyramids, for instance, were more than 4,000 years old. That was 400 centuries!

Also, he knew that the English got much of their wealth from their colonies, especially from India. Napoleon reasoned that if he conquered Egypt he would gain a foothold in the east. It wasn't far from Egypt to India. If he could capture Egypt, he could then go on to invade India. And if he conquered India, England would fall and France would be unstoppable.

He kept his plans for Egypt top secret. If Admiral Nelson had caught him sailing from France to Alexandria, he would have been in big trouble. The French fleet had 13 large battleships to protect them, but against Nelson how many was enough? Napoleon was also carrying a very precious cargo. Along with the thousands of soldiers and horses, he had brought along 500 of France's top scientists.

Since his childhood, Napoleon had been fascinated by how things worked. He grew up to believe that knowledge was the most important thing in the world. He knew Egypt, with its ancient history, would be a wonderful place to learn new things. For Napoleon, the fight against ignorance would always be just as important as the art of war. So he brought astronomers and doctors, physicists and mathematicians, architects and mapmakers. They would help him find out everything he could about Egypt. One of the scientists' first jobs, he said to himself, would be to look into these strange visions of water in the desert.

Luckily, the French expedition arrived safely in Egypt. Admiral Nelson was nowhere to be seen, but Napoleon had a feeling he wasn't far away. After offloading all their equipment and capturing the coastal town of Alexandria, the French army started the march to Cairo. Ahead of them Napoleon sent 700 Turkish slaves he had found being held captive in Alexandria. They were released on condition that they travelled throughout Egypt with letters to the local people from Napoleon. The letters, written in Arabic, said: "We have come to liberate and build, not oppress or destroy. Resistance is futile."

Now in Europe, a march of 120 miles was no big deal. A big army could expect to cover the distance in two or three weeks. Across the desert, 120 miles was a very different story. There was no water. There was no food. There was just the blazing sun and hour after hour of heat and dust. Walking through the sand was like wading through hot treacle. The soft sand sucked at the feet and shoes, drawing out a person's strength. Sometimes it felt to the soldiers as if they were walking on the same spot for hour after hour.

Eventually, after two terrible months, Napoleon found himself a stone's throw from Egypt's capital city, Cairo. He could see the minarets, or towers, of the city mosques in the distance. He could hear the Muslim priests, the muezzins, calling the faithful to prayer from the top of the towers. In the shadow of the ancient pyramids on the outskirts of the city, the French soldiers at last faced the Egyptian defenders. The Battle of the Pyramids was about to begin.

The French soldiers stared in awe at their opponents – 20,000 foot soldiers ranged before them. Napoleon remembered the foreign people he'd seen in the fairs of Paris, but nothing could have prepared him for this: row upon row of Arabs, Coptics and Abyssinians dressed in robes and turbans and carrying all sorts of weapons, from muskets to curved swords. Floating not far off on the waters of the Nile was a large fleet of Arab gunboats. Forty cannon were pointed in their direction. But what gripped the attention of Napoleon most was the 10,000 Mameluke horsemen.

Napoleon had never seen anything quite like them. They were magnificent. They wore elaborate silks embroidered with gold and silver. They each carried a rifle, a long, curved scimitar sword, a shotgun and four pistols. Their horses neighed in anticipation, and scuffed the hard sand with their hooves. Their leader, Mourad-Bey, came out of his huge colourful tent with a flourish, mounted his horse and looked on the scene with pleasure. Today, he mused, the Mameluke scimitars would eat French flesh.

Napoleon moved his dust-covered, miserable, thirsty men into squares, 300 yards across and 50 yards deep. These were called "Battalion squares". This was a common technique used on the battlefields of Europe. It clustered the soldiers into tightly packed groups and enabled them to take turns firing their muskets. Napoleon rode out in front of his troops and trotted down the line of battalion squares.

"Soldiers," he shouted, pointing at the pyramids, "today 40 centuries are looking down on you." He called on them to find the courage and pride to fight for France and for glory. As usual, they were inspired by the little general. They would die for him and for France.

It was then that the Mameluke horsemen charged. The earth shook with the rumbling of hooves. A great cloud of dust rose into the desert sky. The horses and their riders came pouring over the dunes like an angry sea, bubbling and spitting over the rocks. Shouting, the horsemen spurred their steeds on at full pelt toward the French ranks: 10,000 horsemen in billowing robes covered in jewels. They seemed able to ride and shoot each of their guns without breaking stride. The gold on their saddles and clothes glinted in the sun. The French soldiers looked on in total amazement and fear as the Mameluke horsemen drew closer and closer.

But the Mamelukes were no match for the battle-trained French regiments with their cannon, their new muskets and their clever little general. Caught between the battalion squares, they were cut to ribbons. The Battle of the Pyramids lasted only a few hours. The glorious Mameluke horsemen were left bleeding in the sand and the French army was victorious again. By early September, the French flag was flying from the highest minarets in Cairo.

At first, Napoleon was a bit disappointed by what he found in Egypt. He expected treasures like the statues, paintings and artwork he had plundered in Italy, but he didn't find any. He found only old stone temples and carved rock. He hoped for gold, silver or cash, but there wasn't much. He needed thousands of horses for his cavalry and to help pull his guns, but there weren't any around. Instead some of his soldiers learned how to ride camels. He planned to build forts and outposts, but there was no wood in the desert.

However, he did manage to establish the Institute of Egypt for Arts and Sciences. And it didn't take long before his astronomers, mathematicians and scientists started making amazing discoveries.

One of the institute's first tasks, set for it by Napoleon, was to investigate the strange disappearing water phenomenon they had seen during the march in the desert. The water visions were dubbed "mirages" and were found to be caused by the effect of the intense heat rising off the sand.

Napoleon's scientists and artists roamed Egypt recording the features of the terrain, the size of village populations and the distances between towns. They drew accurate maps, measured the depths of canals and rivers, examined the stars and inspected the monuments. They even discovered the famous Rosetta Stone. The Rosetta Stone was the key which unlocked the secret language of ancient Egypt and the pyramids. The stone held a message carved in three languages. As one of these languages was the mysterious Egyptian alphabet called hieroglyphics, the scientists could work out from the other two languages what the hieroglypics said. Until the Rosetta Stone was discovered, no one knew what the carvings on the walls of the pyramids had meant. Thanks to Napoleon, the secret was out.

On August 1, 1798, only a few months after Napoleon had arrived in Cairo, he received some very, very bad news. When he had first landed in Egypt, he had had a nagging feeling that Admiral Nelson wasn't far away. He was right.

Two days after Napoleon and his soldiers had set off on the long march to Cairo, Admiral Nelson had found the French fleet moored near where they had landed the French army, in Aboukir Bay.

Rear-Admiral Sir Horatio Nelson was a shining star in his country's navy and probably the best seaman of his age. A captain at 20, Nelson had lost an eye in a

battle off Corsica and an arm off Tenerife. He had won a knighthood after the Battle of Cape St Vincent and been promoted to Rear-Admiral in 1797. He was a brilliant sailor and leader who had shown his courage and cleverness time and again.

"What happened?" asked Napoleon.

"The French fleet is lost," the messenger said.

"How many ships remain?" said Napoleon.

"Only four, General."

"How many men were lost?"

"1,700, General. Three thousand have been taken prisoner."

Napoleon looked deeply pained. Disaster. How on earth was he going to get this army home?

The news of the loss of Napoleon's fleet at the Battle of Aboukir Bay spread quickly around the world. The little general had seemed unbeatable in Italy. Now he had suffered his first big setback. Even though Napoleon himself wasn't at Aboukir Bay, he had lost his fleet. The English were delighted. With no ships, the chances of Napoleon invading the British Isles were much more remote. The reputation of Rear Admiral Nelson grew even more.

Realising he was stranded in Egypt, Napoleon busied himself with making the country easier to live in. He built roads, dredged canals, put up new windmills and even introduced a postal service. He put Egypt's businesses in order by issuing licenses to shops and restaurants and by establishing chambers of commerce. Napoleon ordered his scientific institute to look into purifying water from the Nile and into winemaking. He set up chemistry and physics laboratories, workshops, a huge library and he built printing presses. It was during this time in one of Napoleon's laboratories that the word "virus" was coined.

But, while Napoleon did much to uplift the people of Egypt, he could also be extremely brutal to those who opposed him. The Egyptians, naturally, didn't want Napoleon and his army living in their country, and they did what they could to make things difficult. They killed French soldiers and stole weapons and equipment. In return, Napoleon used terror to try and keep them quiet. He beheaded spies and rebellious villagers. He put their heads on poles and paraded them through the streets. He took children away from their parents as punishment.

One day, Napoleon did something especially horrible. He was leading a small army of French soldiers from Egypt to the neighbouring country of Syria. He wanted to expand the territory under his command and conquer Syria too. On the way, Napoleon's forces came across the town of Jaffa. The town was defended by 2,500 Turkish soldiers. On seeing the scary French army approaching, the Turks agreed they didn't want to die defending Jaffa. So they decided to surrender. They put their weapons down and held their arms up in surrender and marched out of the town.

Napoleon was expecting a battle, not 2,500 prisoners. He didn't know what to do with them. He didn't have enough food or water for them and he didn't have a prison to put them in. He certainly couldn't take them along with him. And because Turkey was friendly with England, they couldn't just be set free because they were enemy soldiers.

Napoleon thought long and hard about his problem. Finally, he could see no other way. He called his senior aide, Captain Marmont, to his tent.

"I'm afraid we have no option. We have to get rid of the Turks," said Napoleon. "Take them to where nobody will see and kill them."

"All of them?" asked Captain Marmont.

"All of them," replied Napoleon.

With that, the 2,500 Turkish soldiers were marched to a remote beach not far from Jaffa. Once they had reached a place with nobody in sight, all 2,500 men were bayoneted or shot by French soldiers until not a single Turk remained alive.

People did find out, of course. They usually do. It wasn't long before all of Europe was talking of Napoleon's cruelty. The killings added a dark chapter to Napoleon's story, perhaps the darkest chapter of all. The slaughtering of thousands of unarmed men was a terrible thing to do. Napoleon knew as much, and regretted it for the rest of his life. He regretted it all the more when the attempt to conquer Syria failed and all those lives had been lost for nothing.

It was around this time that Napoleon learned from some French newspapers brought to him in Cairo that there was more trouble at home. The French armies that had done so well in Italy under his command had started losing again. They had been beaten in Germany, Switzerland and even in Italy itself. While Napoleon had been in Egypt, England, Russia and Austria had joined forces to attack the French.

Napoleon was beside himself with anger. How could the French government allow this to happen? He had been away barely a year and suddenly everything he had won looked set to be lost. He decided to return to France at once.

CHAPTER 9 – HOMEWARD BOUND

Aboukir Bay, 17 August, 1799: Napoleon pulled his cloak tightly around him and held on to the side of the row boat. He watched the Egyptian coast shrink back into the darkness. It was midnight and Napoleon felt bad. He felt bad that he was leaving his army behind. He had not even told the man who would take over from him and take charge of the French army, General Jean Kleber, that he was leaving. But secrecy was vital. There were spies everywhere. If the English heard Napoleon was leaving Egypt, Admiral Nelson would be waiting for him. Napoleon also felt bad that he was leaving Egypt with so many things still to do. His dream of using this campaign as a springboard to India would have to wait. "France needs me," Napoleon thought to himself. "I must return."

The small boat pulled up to the side of one of the two waiting frigates. Napoleon stood, swaying in the swell, and reached out for the rope ladder. He climbed up and on to the deck. He wondered, as he lay on his bunk, if Admiral Nelson was anywhere near. How Nelson would love to catch him on a small frigate, alone on the Mediterranean Sea. Would he fire all his cannon and sink him, or would he capture him and take him back to London in chains? Napoleon didn't fancy either. He snuggled deeper into his bed and closed his eyes. The rocking ship sailed off into the night, hugging close to the African coast to avoid enemy cruisers.

The journey seemed to take forever. The wind seemed always to be against them. The days dragged on and on. Napoleon was desperate to get back to France. All he could do was wait. To pass the time he played card games or chess with his officers. Nobody like playing games with Napoleon. He wasn't very good at chess and he always cheated at cards.

His officers got quite cross when Napoleon cheated and then took their money. But what could they say? He was General Napoleon. In any case, Napoleon usually gave their money back later when nobody was looking.

On the way back to France, the small fleet stopped and anchored in Ajaccio harbour, Corsica. Napoleon was home. For six days, he explored the island. He met up with old friends and distant relatives and visited the places he loved. He rode through the maquis and smelled the orange groves. They were special days. He knew as he took in all the sights and smells and sounds of Corsica that this would probably be the last time he would visit. He was right.

After six days, the two frigates set off once more. It wasn't far from Ajaccio to France. When their ship was only a few miles from the French coast, the lookout on the highest mast shouted: "Enemy ships to starboard, enemy ships to starboard!" Napoleon and his officers rushed to the bridge deck. The little general looked through his spyglass. There, not far off at all, were the sails of a whole squadron of English battleships. Finally, Nelson had caught up with him.

Napoleon swung his spyglass round and looked straight ahead, toward where the two French frigates were sailing as fast as they could. There was the French port of Frejus. It seemed about the same distance away as the English fleet. Would they make it? Napoleon wondered. Could they really have got this close to home, only to be captured by the English? Would this be how Napoleon's story ended?

Luckily, the wind, for once, was in Napoleon's favour. The two frigates managed to keep a good distance between themselves and the English warships. Before long, the French sailors were all sighing with relief, slapping backs and shaking hands as they sailed into Frejus harbour. Nelson and his squadron turned away. Napoleon had eluded the famous English admiral once more.

It had been about a year and a half since Napoleon and his fleet had set out on their expedition to Egypt. Napoleon knew from the newspapers he had been given that things had deteriorated in France. He wondered how much worse the situation had become in the weeks it had taken him to get home. He got a bad feeling when a row-boat paddled out to the frigate. It stopped 50 yards from where Napoleon's ship had thrown anchor.

"You may not come ashore," a man yelled. His face was wrapped in a scarf.

"Why not?" shouted back the captain of the frigate.

"The plague. We don't want the plague here in Frejus. You must wait there until we are sure you don't have it on board."

"We don't have the plague, but we do have General Bonaparte aboard," shouted the captain.

"General Bonaparte himself?" shouted the man.

"The very same."

"I will ask the port captain and return." With that, the scarved man turned his boat around and paddled back to the jetty. Before long, the port captain rowed out to the frigate. He climbed aboard and, on meeting Napoleon, agreed that the men on the frigate could disembark.

"As a special favour to such a famous man," said the port captain, smiling as he shook Napoleon's hand.

So on the 9th of October, 1799, Napoleon finally set foot on French soil. Almost immediately, he climbed into a carriage and set off for Paris. On the way, one of his officers brought him up to date with recent events.

"The treasury is out of money again. All public building projects have been put on hold. The army has not been paid," the young officer said. Napoleon nodded grimly.

"There is fighting in many parts of France. People want a king back on the throne. The police don't have enough men or equipment to arrest the trouble-makers."

"What of Austria, Prussia and Russia?" asked Napoleon.

"There is talk of invasion, General. Soldiers from England, Naples, Portugal and Turkey have joined with Russia and Austria. They have vowed to crush France. Even now they are building their forces on our borders."

Napoleon nodded, his face even grimmer than before. "What have you done with the country I left so powerful?" Napoleon muttered to himself.

But as they spoke, Napoleon could hear cheering along the roadside. He was desperate to hear all the news, but every few seconds a fresh round of clapping and cheering broke out.

"What is all the cheering about?" Napoleon asked the officer.

"They are cheering for you, General."

Napoleon looked out the window. Smiling, happy people called his name and waved. "Napoleon is back!"

they shouted. "Hurrah for Napoleon!"

The closer Napoleon got to Paris, the more people came out to cheer and clap and shout. Even in small towns, people lit the streets with candles and hung flowers from windows.

All the way to Paris, for the entire six-day journey, Napoleon was welcomed with joy and fanfare. Suddenly France's big problems didn't seem so big. Napoleon was home at last. In Paris itself, Napoleon was treated as France's conquering hero. Thousands of Parisians lined the streets. The city itself was lit up in his honour. The French forgave him for losing the fleet at Aboukir Bay. They were just pleased to have him back ready to win more battles and save them from chaos and from foreign enemies.

None were more pleased to see Napoleon than a very powerful group of French politicians, led by Napoleon's brother, Lucien. Lucien had turned out to be a very clever, well-liked man. Since the Bonaparte family had been booted out of Corsica ten years previously, he had grown up to be an important official in the government. Lucien persuaded this powerful group that his brother, Napoleon, was the perfect man to take charge of France. As they watched Napoleon ride in glory into Paris, the government officials agreed that perhaps it was time that this popular, skilful, little general played a bigger role. Perhaps it *was* time for him to lead France. What did they have to lose? Things were looking bad for France, after all. There was chaos inside the country and armies lining up outside. Yes, maybe Napoleon's time had come...

When Josephine heard that Napoleon had returned, she was horrified. She was dining with the president Louis Gohier when one of her ladies-in-waiting whispered in her ear.

"Your husband is almost in Paris, madame."

Josephine leapt up at once.

"You will have to excuse me, President Gohier, but I must return immediately to greet my husband," she said.

Josephine rushed to her coach. "Which road will he be coming from?" she asked her lady-in-waiting.

"I think on the western road, madame."

"Coachman," cried Josephine, "take us to the western road. We must intercept my husband's carriage. Leave at once." With that, Josephine's coach sped off.

As she sat in the jolting coach, she rehearsed what she would say to her husband. She knew he would be angry with her: "My dear husband, my love, please ignore the horrible rumours about me. I love you and only you. Now that you are home, let us be together and not worry about the past."

She wondered if Napoleon had already heard about her affair with the dashing Hippolyte Charles or with President Gohier or indeed about any of the liaisons she had enjoyed in the past year and a half. She also wondered when she would tell him about the huge debts she needed him to pay off for her. She had bought some jewellery and clothes, that was true. She had also shopped for shawls, dresses, hats and shoes. She was the wife of an important general, after all. She didn't know exactly how many things she had, but she was sure Napoleon would pay for it all when he got home.

In fact, when someone eventually added up what was in Josephine's wardrobe, they counted 666 winter dresses, 230 summer ones, 60 cashmere shawls and, perhaps surprisingly, just two pairs of knickers.

The coachman, unfortunately, chose the wrong road. For two days, Josephine travelled up and down looking for Napoleon. He was nowhere to be seen. Eventually she returned home to her small house in Paris. There was Napoleon's carriage.

"Napoleon, Napoleon," she called. "Where are you, my love?" But Napoleon had locked himself in their bedroom. He had heard what Josephine had been up to while he was away and he was furious.

"Please, please open up," Josephine begged. "Please, Napoleon."

"Go away," shouted Napoleon. "I am divorcing you. Pack your bags and go away."

Josephine was devastated. She pleaded with Napoleon but he refused to listen. For two days she waited at the doorway, calling to Napoleon, pleading with him, promising to be faithful from now on. But Napoleon would not listen or open the door. At her wits' end, Josephine asked her two children, Eugène and Hortense, to knock on the door and speak with Napoleon. Napoleon loved Eugène, who was one of his aides, and his daughter Hortense was gentle and sweet. Napoleon opened his door.

The following morning, Napoleon's brother, Lucien, arrived at Josephine's house. He knew there had been trouble between his brother and Josephine. In fact, it had been him who had told Napoleon all the details. But he had some urgent business to discuss with his brother. It was so urgent he could not wait for their marriage problems to sort themselves out. Lucien jumped off his horse, gave the reins to a servant and knocked on Josephine's front door.

"Ah, monsieur Lucien Bonaparte, please come in," said the doorman. "Your brother is waiting for you. Please follow me."

Lucien entered the house, and was shown straight into Josephine's bedroom, where Napoleon and Josephine lay in bed in each other's arms.

"Ah, Lucien, how are you?" asked Napoleon, grinning.

"I see all is well," replied Lucien.

"Yes, we are happy again," said Napoleon.

"We have important business; can we talk?" said Lucien.

"Now?" asked Napoleon.

"Now," replied Lucien.

"Very well," said Napoleon, kissing Josephine on the cheek, clambering out of bed and pulling on a nightgown.

Napoleon and his brother sat down in comfortable chairs and looked across at one another.

"I have an offer for you, my brother," said Lucien. "I represent a powerful group who think you should be leading France. We want you to be one of three consuls, the first consul in fact. What do you say?"

"Who is 'we'?" asked Napoleon.

"Joseph Fouché, minister of police, Admiral Bruix, the head of the navy, Monsieur Talleyrand, who was the foreign minister until recently, as well as several high-ranking army officers and politicians."

"An impressive group. So you are leading a coup, Lucien, and you want me to be part of it?" asked Napoleon.

"Yes," said Lucien. "What have you got to lose?" Lucien had a point, Napoleon thought to himself. At that moment, Napoleon had no army. His soldiers were still in Egypt and had no way of getting home. He didn't really want to go and lead the French Army of Italy again, he'd already done that. He wasn't sure Lucien's coup would work, but what other options did he have? After quickly thinking things through, Napoleon agreed that maybe he would enjoy leading France.

"All right, Lucien. I accept. What is the plan?"

"In a few weeks, senior officials in the government will issue two decrees. The first decree will move the government to an old château on the outskirts of Paris called St Cloud. We will tell everyone we are doing that for security reasons. The second decree will declare you commander in chief of the troops in and around Paris. Once we've got the government where we want them and put you in charge of the army, the rest will be easy."

Napoleon nodded in satisfaction. It was a good plan. But would it work?

On the 9th of November, 1799 (or the 18th of Brumaire in the Revolutionary calendar), the two decrees were issued and the plotters began to put their plan into place. There was much confusion about moving the government from Paris to St Cloud. In the midst of it all, Lucien, Napoleon and a brigade of soldiers marched in to a meeting of the government and announced they had seized power. The government was furious, but what could they do? Trapped in a château on the outskirts of Paris, surrounded by soldiers, they could do nothing but agree to step aside. In their places, three "consuls" were appointed to rule France. Napoleon was named as the most powerful, the First Consul. He had moved, just like that, from being a successful general to being the real ruler of France.

A few months after the coup of the 18th Brumaire, in the summer of 1800, Napoleon was riding in his carriage from Josephine's house to his office at the Tuileries Palace. So much had happened in just a few months. He knew people had been angry at how their elected government had been kicked out of power. But it was obvious to him now that the people of France were happy to have him, First Consul Napoleon, as their leader. He had restored order to the capital. He had placed his friends into important positions. France was stable once more. Then, when people had settled back into their routines, he had led his armies north to see off the foreign threat.

First on his list had been winning back the territory that had been taken from him in northern Italy. Once more, his tactics took the enemy by surprise. Nobody expected for a minute that he, Napoleon, would lead his army right over the snow-covered Alps to launch an attack. Everyone knew you couldn't pull a wagon or a heavy gun through deep snow. But, as usual, he had a plan. Napoleon didn't believe anything was impossible. He took his guns off their wheels, placed them in hollowed out trees and dragged them over the Alps like sleds. The French Army, once again, started winning battles. One of the most important was the defeat he handed to the Austrians at the Battle of Marengo on the 14th June, 1800. Soon, he had won back all the land that had been lost, and gained more.

Napoleon was back and France was strong again. But

there remained so much to do. Napoleon gazed out of the window. He was so sad at the state of Paris. The narrow streets were muddy. The houses looked like they were about to fall down. Napoleon couldn't think how anyone could find their way around Paris. Few of the streets had names. Dark passages led to blind alleys. There was no lighting. In the few streets that had flagstones, these were uneven and broken. Napoleon was grateful it wasn't raining. When it rained, the roads turned to a sticky, black sludge that no carriage could pass down. The rainwater poured straight from the long gutter pipes onto the road and mixed up the sewerage and the rubbish. It was disgusting.

Napoleon noticed that empty pedestals stood in many squares where statues of the King used to be. And the beautiful houses, once owned by nobles, now stood ruined and empty. Their owners had fled. Their houses had been robbed and anything valuable taken. Even the courtyard gates were gone. It was as if the houses were missing their front teeth.

Near the River Seine, Napoleon noticed the dreadful smell. The river water was awful and unhealthy. Floating mills and washhouse boats pumped their filth straight into the Seine. No wonder people got sick when they drunk Paris's water. Around the next corner, Napoleon's carriage came to a sudden stop.

"What's the hold-up?" he asked the driver.

"Cattle, General," the driver replied.

Napoleon leaned out of the carriage window and looked ahead. There was a herd of 30 oxen being led down a Parisian street by a few men and their dogs. They were off to be slaughtered at the market. But there was no slaughterhouse. They would kill them and cut them up right there on the street.

Napoleon decided he must do something about Paris. He wanted his capital city to be beautiful, the talk of Europe. He didn't want it to be a run-down sewer full of dead cows and dirty water. He wanted new roads and tunnels, bridges and hospitals, canals and orphanages. He wanted Paris to have a university. He wanted it to be lined with wide streets, gardens and grand monuments. And it wouldn't stop there. There was so much he wanted to change, not just in Paris but in France. He wanted a new system of laws and a national Bank. He wanted to sort the schools out, get science and the arts going and even improve relations with the Church. He also wanted a Bank of France so that everyone's francs were worth the same. He was determined to do all these things. One day when he was gone, he wanted people to look at France and at Paris and say: "There is Napoleon's work."

When his carriage pulled up to the Tuileries Palace, Napoleon noticed that even here, too, there were signs of disrepair. There were dozens of small holes and even some big craters in the walls where cannonballs and bullets had once hit. They must have come from years ago when Napoleon had beaten General Danican and his Royalist army. Why hadn't the holes been patched up? So much had to be done.

Many French people were proud and excited to have Napoleon as their First Consul. Whenever he rode through the streets of Paris with his regiments, huge crowds gathered to catch a glimpse of the little general. Men, women and children dashed between the horses' legs to touch the gilding on his saddle and to see the face of the First Consul in his scarlet coat. Those who had seen him ran on ahead to see him again. So popular was Napoleon that the people of France voted for him to be appointed First Consul for life. He accepted this position on 15th August, 1802, his 33rd birthday. When Napoleon restored popular holidays, such as New Year's Day and the Paris Carnival, and lit up the sky with fireworks on special occasions, the people's joy was great indeed.

But there were still many who hated Napoleon. They swore to get rid of him once and for all. For them, he was the man keeping the Bourbon monarchy from their rightful throne. He was the one threatening Europe.

On Christmas Eve of 1800, Napoleon and Josephine were making their way to the Opera in Paris for a performance of Haydn's *The Creation*. Moments after the Bonapartes' carriage had passed, a huge bomb went off. The bomb was made up of a whole barrel full of explosives. When it blew up, it shook the whole city. Twenty-two people died that day while a further 57 bystanders were wounded by bits of flying metal and splinters of wood. More than 40 houses were damaged. A very shaken Napoleon and Josephine only narrowly escaped with their lives.

The bomb made Napoleon think: what will happen if I die? Who will take over from me? Will all this be for nothing?

CHAPTER 10 – KIDNAPPED!

Ettenheim, Baden, March 1804: Few people noticed the small force of a dozen, heavily armed French soldiers. They didn't say where they were going and nobody dared ask. Even when they secretly crossed the Rhine and rode east, their movements were common enough. Though the Duchy of Baden was independent, small detachments of French soldiers moving around the countryside were hardly rare in those days. They might have been delivering important mail or carrying the diplomatic pouch. Certainly nobody who caught sight of them would have guessed in a million years what they were up to. But their mission was deadly serious and would begin to change the face of Europe.

They rode by cover of darkness to a sprawling country residence deep in the heart of Baden. Here the 32-year-old Duke of Enghien was entertaining his mistress. The Duke was an important member of the exiled French royal family. He was a cousin of the guillotined king. He chose not to live in France and kept to himself. He stayed well away from the gossiping and dangers of Paris – but not far enough.

When the French soldiers arrived at the estate, they split up to block the exits. Nobody would be allowed to escape. Then a small group of them rode into the estate and hammered on the door.

"We have come for the Duke," they called.

The Duke came to the front entrance. "What do you want?" he asked.

"We arrest you in the name of the First Consul of France," they replied.

"But you can't arrest me here," said the Duke. "We are in a neutral country. We are in Baden."

"We have our orders," replied the soldiers. "You are to come with us."

"This is kidnapping. You will not hear the end of this, that I can promise you," said the Duke. He threw on a hat and cloak, mounted his horse and was led off into the night.

The soldiers took the Duke of Enghien back across the Rhine and into France. Then they rode to a castle, the Château Vincennes, near Paris. Here, in a cold, draughty room in the castle, the Duke was put on trial.

"You are charged with plotting to kill the First Consul, Napoleon Bonaparte. How do you plead?" he was asked.

"Not guilty. I had nothing to do with it," replied the Duke.

But the trial had been fixed. Napoleon wanted to make an example of the Duke.

"This court finds you guilty. The sentence is death."

In the early hours of March 21, 1804, the Duke of Enghien was led to the moat of the château. A grave had already been dug. He was told to stand up against the wall of the château. He was then shot dead by a firing squad.

Why had he shot the Duke? Because Napoleon was tired of people trying to kill him. Close to 30 times, attempts had been made on his life. They were usually planned by the Comte d'Artois, the brother of Louis, the next in line to the French throne. They were also usually paid for by the English. One man had come at him with a knife. Another had blown up a whole street in Paris. They had tried to poison him, shoot him, capture him. They thought of all sorts of ways to get rid of him. This would only end, Napoleon thought, when he had taught them a lesson. He had been pretty tough when he needed to be. Once he had rounded up 200 French nobles accused of plotting against him. He had put them and their families on ships and sent them for ever to distant islands. But he was tired now. These constant attacks had to be stopped. The Duke of Enghien was planning to kill Napoleon. At least that's what he had been told. Well then the Duke of Enghien would learn his lesson the hard way. Perhaps others would not be so hasty, Napoleon thought to himself.

But, six months after the Duke's killing, Napoleon was amazed that people were still so angry with him about it. News of the Duke's death had caused fury in every court in Europe. Emperors, kings and nobles cursed it as the work of a bloodthirsty tyrant. They called Napoleon "Boney, the Corsican Ogre". Europe's royal families and aristocrats swore to bring his rule to an end. "We must do everything we can to be rid of this pest," they shouted. The Russian Tsar, Alexander, who had been friendly with Napoleon, was especially angry. He could not forgive Napoleon for executing a noble in cold blood. His own father had been killed just the same way. Tsar Alexander decided that he would not speak to Napoleon again. He also stopped his diplomats from talking to Napoleon's diplomats. This was a big step in those days, as it would be now. Instead, the Tsar began to talk with the Austrians and the English about joining forces once more against the dreaded little French general.

But Napoleon still thought they were making a big thing out of nothing. In any case, that had been six months ago. Today was much too important to worry about old news. Today, Napoleon would be joining the ranks of those who most hated him. Today, Napoleon would be crowned as the Emperor of France. He looked at the clothes that had been set out for his coronation. There was a formal red velvet coat richly hemmed with gold and decorated with bees. He had chosen bees for his personal symbol. He had always liked them and they had once been the symbol for an ancient French King. There before him was the white plumed hat he would wear. Next to it was the sword with a huge diamond mounted in the hilt that he would fix to his side.

He would certainly look the part of an emperor.

As he prepared for the big day, Napoleon was sure he had done the right thing. He knew there would be a few people who would criticize him for bringing back the monarchy to France. But this was different to the Bourbon monarchy. The Bourbons had just taken the throne. He, Napoleon, had asked the French people if that was what they wanted, and they had all said yes! Three and a half million people had voted for him to be Emperor of France. Only a few thousand had voted against him. So it was the French people who had made Napoleon emperor. They trusted him to continue with the ideals of the revolution that had thrown out the Bourbons. And he would. He believed in equality, liberty and fraternity. Of course he also believed in a French empire that would stretch from one side of the globe to the other. And he believed in his own destiny to lead France and, when he was old, to hand on his vision to his son, and to his son's sons.

A slight problem was that he didn't have any sons. In fact, he and Josephine had been unable to have any children at all. This made Napoleon think long and hard about whether or not to make Josephine the Empress. After all, he might have to find someone who could give him children. How was he to continue the Bonaparte line with no children? Josephine also continued to make him angry with her lovers and her debts. She tried to make things better by forcing shops to cut their bills by half. Only then did she post them to him for payment. But the bills were still much too high and he was always getting angry. When Napoleon got angry, Josephine cried and sulked.

Napoleon couldn't help chuckling when he recalled losing his temper so badly with Josephine that he had sliced off the tops of her favourite flowers with his riding crop. Once he had even taken his musket and shot at Josephine's exotic black swans. But Napoleon didn't want talk of divorce to spoil his coronation day. When the time came, he would find a new, young wife to bear him sons. In the meantime, he was determined to put on the best royal show in the world. He would make Josephine his empress today and worry about tomorrow, tomorrow.

Just then, Josephine walked in. She looked exquisite. She wore a white satin gown trimmed with silver and gold. Round her neck, a diamond necklace glinted in the light of the chandelier. A jewelled girdle sparkled at her waist. Diamonds and pearls were threaded into her hair. She took Napoleon's breath away. She looked fit to be a queen. In a few hours, she would be one.

"Shall we go and get our crowns, madame?" asked Napoleon, bowing his head and then holding out an arm.

"I am ready, my Emperor," replied Josephine, curtseying and slipping her gloved hand around his elbow.

With that, the two left the Tuileries Palace, arm-in-arm. They climbed on to a carriage that had been specially decorated for the day. It had glass sides and was topped by four silver eagles. In the eagles' wings was a crown. Before their carriage was rank upon rank of smartly dressed horsemen.

Napoleon and Josephine settled into their chairs and their carriage proceeded to leave the palace. Behind it, 29 other carriages full of their family, friends and ministers followed them. It took an age to reach Notre Dame Cathedral. Josephine had to look twice because she didn't recognize the cathedral. Something was different. Then she realised that a massive canvas had been put up around the cathedral and painted to make it look like St Peter's in Rome. It was as if they were getting crowned at the Vatican itself. Of course, the Pope himself would be waiting for them in the cathedral. He had come specially to bless them and their crowns. Now nobody could question their right to the French throne. Thousands of people watched the carriage roll past. "*Vive L'Empereur!*" they shouted, "Long live the Emperor!"

"I believe Paris is so full of people coming to the coronation that the hotels and guesthouses are full," said

Josephine. "Many of our citizens will be sleeping in tents tonight."

"Yes, but what a party they will have," laughed Napoleon.

Watched by the Pope, foreign visitors and by the most important citizens in France, Napoleon walked up the altar steps, picked up the imperial crown and placed it on his own head. It was 2nd December, 1804 and Napoleon had become an Emperor. Then, Napoleon crowned Josephine as Empress-Queen. During the ceremony, Napoleon leaned over and said to his brother Joseph: "If our father could see us now."

Josephine and Napoleon, wearing their new crowns, then returned to the Tuileries palace. They went a very long route that was lit by thousands of torches held by cheering citizens. Gravel was put on the roads to make it easier for the royal procession.

"*Vive L'Empereur!*" the people shouted as Napoleon and Josephine rolled past, smiling and waving. The festivities went on for two weeks.

Back at the palace, nothing much changed to signal that Napoleon was now an emperor and not just the First Consul. People said Napoleon had been living like a king for a while now. He had started a new nobility called the legion of honour. These were people to whom he awarded titles and money. One of the lucky ones was his old friend from military school, Alexander des Mazis.

Napoleon discovered that Alexander was penniless and living in exile. Napoleon insisted on bringing him home and gave him an important position. Napoleon never forgot his old friends.

Napoleon kept his office in the palace pretty simple. There were a couple of desks, bookcases, a cupboard, a settee, a fireplace and a mantel holding a bronze statue of one of his heroes, Frederick the Great of Prussia, riding a horse. But beyond the doors to his study, the Tuileries was like a real monarch's castle. There were teams of chefs to prepare elaborate meals. There were secretaries, footmen, coachmen, huntsmen and librarians. Napoleon had a personal valet to shave and dress him, four chamberlains, a governor of the palace, two interpreters and a military office headed by four generals. Josephine herself had four ladies-in-waiting.

Even before he was Emperor, people couldn't just pop in to see the little general. They had to make appointments. There were strict rules about what you should wear when you went to see Napoleon, and about how you should address him. The military uniforms worn by his staff in the early days were replaced with courtly outfits, stockings and all the trimmings. Napoleon himself kept wearing a simple, military uniform and on occasion swore like a trooper. But those close to him saw how he was changing. It was as if France was no longer enough. Napoleon had a much bigger prize in sight. He dreamed that all Europe would one day be united under French rule: one land, one law, one currency, one court, one government and one ruler.

While the coronation party continued in Paris, Napoleon was getting restless. He knew he must soon return to the coast where his armies were gathering to invade England. As soon as he could, he bade farewell to Josephine, called his officers and staff together, jumped into his carriage and travelled east. After a few days he reached Boulogne on the French north coast. He might be an Emperor now but he had work to do.

And so it was that he waited on the high cliffs of Boulogne with a spyglass pointed at England over the water. Each day he stood, gazing out in hope. "When will Admiral Villeneuve come?" he muttered to himself. "Where are you, you villain?"

But Villeneuve never came.

Hundreds of miles away, Villeneuve had changed his mind. He had decided he wouldn't sail back to Boulogne. He didn't really believe Napoleon wanted to invade England. Impossible!

"Napoleon just wants me to be part of some trick to fool the English," he said to himself when he got his orders to sail as fast as he could to the Channel. "Napoleon doesn't have the first idea about how a navy works. It's easy to tell me to outwit Admiral Nelson in a wild chase half way across the world, but not so easy to do. My ships are falling apart. My crews are sick with scurvy and dysentery. The Spanish ships meant to be helping us are in an even worse state than us. I've heard they will mutiny if I order them to sail to England. No, it's ridiculous. There is no way I am sailing to Boulogne." And with that, Admiral Villeneueve sailed his fleet into the safety of the port of Cadiz in Spain.

When he eventually heard what Villeneuve had done, Napoleon was beside himself with fury. "What a navy!" he yelled. "What an admiral!" he shouted. "Bring him home and put him on trial for treason!" Napoleon's plan to invade England was ruined. He knew that far off on the eastern front, the armies of Austria and of Russia were once more preparing to attack France. He thought that if things had gone well with Villeneuve, there would have been time to invade England and still get back to protect his eastern frontier. Now, though, things had changed. In late August, he called in his most senior officer, Marshal Berthier. "Turn the army round and march east," said Napoleon.

"What about the English?" asked Berthier.

"They, my friend, will have to wait," replied Napoleon.

CHAPTER 11 – "THE FINEST EVENING OF MY LIFE"

On the afternoon of 1st December, 1805, Napoleon carried out his final inspection of his army before the Battle of Austerlitz. He was very proud of what he saw. He had built an enormous army. It was now known as the Grand Army and it was by far the biggest single army in the world. Better than that, it was well trained. For months his regiments had drilled and practised, intent on winning glory in England. Napoleon had introduced many new ideas. He'd established the Imperial Guard, an elite group of soldiers intended to protect the Emperor. He had created mini-armies within the Grand Army. Each mini army consisted of a battery of artillery, a small group of cavalry and a force of infantry. The beauty of this idea was the speed with which he could move these mini-armies around the countryside. They held up and confused the larger enemy battalions, sometimes for crucial hours.

As he rode among the soldiers, Napoleon ignored their

scruffy dress and muddy boots. It was their weapons and equipment to which he paid special attention. "What have you done with your scouring rod?" he shouted at one soldier.

"I, er, I think I may have left it behind, Emperor," the poor soldier said.

"You've lost it?" screamed Napoleon. "Admit it then, you f***er," and off he stormed.

The soldiers feared and loved Napoleon. No other general used foul language quite like he did. He paused every now and then to swop a joke with a soldier. From time to time he would notice a veteran he had seen at other battles. "Still with me are you, soldier?" he would call. "Yes, Emperor. As long as I have life in my limbs," they would respond. If Napoleon was in a very good mood, he would pinch the ears of some of them. He looked at his men with great fondness. He knew they would follow him to hell and back. By nightfall, he had made his last plans for the looming battle.

As he returned to his headquarters in the early hours of the following morning, one of the soldiers remembered that 2nd December was the first anniversary of Napoleon's coronation as Emperor.

"*Vive L'Empereur*!" he shouted. Soon cries of "*Vive L'Empereur*!" burst out through the camp and excited soldiers began waving torches and shouting. A pile of straw caught alight and soon the whole French camp was a mass of flame and wild cheering. The Russians and Austrians thought a night attack had begun and rushed to defend themselves. Napoleon was angry at the chaos, but pleased by the joy of his troops. As he finally returned to his tent around 4am, he said to himself: "This is the finest evening of my life."

Napoleon recalled with pleasure the amazing speed with which he had marched his army from Boulogne on the western coast of France all the way to the farthest reaches of his empire in the east. This was classic Napoleon: speed, speed, speed. The little general gathered his troops up in formation, with the infantry on either side of the road, with the cavalry on the outside and the artillery and heavy supply wagons in the centre. Each day the troops began marching before the sun was up at around 4am. They marched right through to midday. Every hour there was a five-minute break during which the soldiers relaxed as music was played on clarinets, flutes and horns. Then, it was back on the road once more. If the men looked sleepy, an order was given to beat the drums.

Napoleon chuckled when he heard one of his soldiers say proudly: "The Emperor makes use of our legs instead of our bayonets."

Surely no army had crossed Europe faster than Napoleon's? In 20 days his troops marched from Boulogne, across France, over the Rhine and into southern Germany. This was quicker than it took the post in those days. So before reports were even received that the French army was on the move, they had already arrived. The speed of the advance caught the Austrian army totally unprepared. When Napoleon's advance guard crossed the River Danube, they found a very surprised group of Austrian officers having their dinner. The officers were meant to be on the lookout for the French army but didn't think for a moment it was anywhere nearby.

How Napoleon laughed when he heard about capturing those surprised Austrian officers. And how Napoleon boiled when he thought about Admiral Villeneuve. All across Europe, as he marched with his army, he fumed about his admiral and thought of ways of taking his revenge. He decided Villeneuve would be brought home to face a trial for cowardice.

Napoleon still didn't give up on being crowned King of England. He even thought that once he had sorted out Russia and Austria, he would turn his attention once more to teaching the English a lesson.

Until he had time to mount a new invasion, he decid-

ed, he would strangle England. He would use the power he had in Europe to build a ring of iron around the British Isles. He would make sure England couldn't trade; he'd take English ships' cargoes and imprison her crews. He would forbid nations to do business with her. He would put in place a ring so tight, a "continental system" as he called it, that it would slowly suck the life out of England's veins. Soon, England would be begging him to sail across the Channel.

But as Napoleon rode east, plotting Villeneuve's downfall and Britain's strangling, a sombre-faced messenger appeared before him. It was just after Napoleon had beaten the first part of Austria's army at the Battle of Ulm, on 21st October, 1805.

"Emperor," the messenger said, "there is news from Admiral Villeneuve."

"Harumpf, that coward," Napoleon muttered as he ripped the seal off the letter. The letter was a message from the Admiral. It said the French fleet had finally left Cadiz. "Took your time," Napoleon said out aloud.

But disaster had befallen Villeneuve. Who had the fleet

met just after leaving the safety of harbour? Admiral Nelson. The letter said the English ships had attacked the French and Spanish fleet just off Cape Trafalgar. Napoleon's entire navy was destroyed. Only a few ships had escaped, including, Napoleon couldn't help but notice, Admiral Villeneuve's.

Napoleon knew now his dream of invading England had gone forever. Admiral Nelson had been killed during the battle at Trafalgar, that was true. But France didn't have a navy any more, so Nelson's job was done. It would be many years before enough ships could be built to even think of invading England. At least Villeneueve had had the decency to kill himself shortly after writing the message. But there was still a Russian army to fight. And Napoleon turned his attention to this rather large obstacle.

It was just before dawn when he took off his boots, pulled back the taffeta curtain around his cot and stretched out for an hour or two of rest. He was too tired to read, but he thought about it for a moment as he looked over at a selection from his battlefield library. Napoleon so loved reading, he refused to travel anywhere, including to war, without having his own library close at hand.

Napoleon had designed the portable library himself. It consisted of 30 mahogany cases full of books. In each case, there were three rows of 33 books each. None of the books had margins so no space was wasted. Each book was between 500 and 600 pages long. All in all, there were some 3,000 volumes. About two thirds of the collection were the memoirs of historical figures and the rest were a mix of novels, plays, poetry and religious books – including the Bible and the Koran. The army never forgot to carry Napoleon's portable library, along with the cannons, the wagons and the equipment.

But on that famous morning, Napoleon didn't read. He closed his eyes and dozed for a few hours. At first light, he was awoken with a shake. He pulled on his boots, his hat and his heavy grey cloak and left the tent. A heavy mist had settled on the ground of Austerlitz. As the sun rose, the peaks of the highest hilltops emerged from a white sea of mist. Beneath the swirling, heavy cloud of moisture, waiting for the battle to begin, were 73,000 Frenchmen with 139 cannon and 89,000 allied, mostly Russian troops with 278 guns. It was one of the heaviest concentrations of men and weaponry seen in any battle of modern history.

At 7am, the two allied emperors opposed to Napoleon rode out to inspect their army. They rode side by side: the Russian Tsar, Alexander, in a black uniform with white plumes in his hat mounted on a bob-tailed chestnut horse, and Emperor Francis of Austria in a white uniform on a black charger. As the two emperors watched, the Russian general Marshal Mikhail Kutuzov gave the order and the vast allied army disappeared into the fog and marched toward Napoleon.

Napoleon stood on a hilltop and waited for them. He had a master plan, as he always did. As he saw the Russian and Austrian troops advance, he began to move his own soldiers like pieces on a chessboard. His plan was to set a tempting trap, lure the allied armies into it, and then crush them. For several hours, the battle seesawed this way and that. One moment, the Russian infantry was advancing, the next the French cavalry was attacking. Napoleon knew that even though he had the biggest army in the world, the combined army of Russians and Austrians was bigger than his. He used his old friend speed to outwit them. He made one French regiment fight in one spot, then pull back and rush somewhere else to fight at another. This made the French army seem bigger than it was.

After several hours, Napoleon knew he had won. He had tempted the Russians and the Austrians into the trap and they had fallen for it. Soon his troops began the destruction of the allied armies. By the end of the day, more than 20,000 men lay dead. That's more people than would fit in a medium-sized soccer stadium. Many, many more were injured, too, in what was one of Europe's most famous battles. You wouldn't want to have been injured in the Napoleonic wars. Medicine then was very, very basic. Usually it meant hacking off an injured leg or arm and hoping for the best. Most of the injured soldiers died a few days later.

In the end, Napoleon and his French army were victorious. The Austrians and the Russians were beaten. "Soldiers, I am pleased with you," Napoleon told his army after the battle. "You have on the day of Austerlitz fulfilled all I expected of your intrepidity; you have decorated your eagles with an immortal glory. An army commanded by the Emperors of Russia and Austria, has, in less than four hours, been either cut up or dispersed... My people will greet you with joy, and it will be enough for you to say: "I was at the battle of Austerlitz," for them to reply, "There goes a warrior!"

As Napoleon signed new peace treaties with his defeated enemies, he could hardly have been happier. After the battle of Austerlitz, he feared no nation's army. He was known throughout the world. He had defeated his enemies. He had rebuilt France. His army was unmatched. Now he had humbled the two most powerful emperors in Europe. He knew there would be further battles ahead, but was sure he was one step closer to ruling all of Europe and, perhaps, all of the world.

CHAPTER 12 –
STORM CLOUDS RISING

Paris, July 1807: "How wonderful it is to be home once more," thought Napoleon, as he rode his horse down the Champs Elysées. Around him were his famous Imperial Guard, marching proudly. They carried the regimental flags or standards captured from enemy armies. People were cheering "*Vive L'Empereur!*"

After many months, the victorious Emperor was back in Paris. Ahead of him, the Arc de Triomphe was being built. What a magnificent monument it will be, Napoleon thought to himself. All around him, the city was celebrating. Cannon boomed from Les Invalides to welcome him. Heralds clad in medieval costume and holding smoking torches called his name. Military bands and spectators jammed the broad avenues.

Things had certainly gone well for the Bonaparte family. They had never been so well placed. Wherever he conquered, Napoleon placed members of his family in charge. Joseph was now the King of Naples. Louis was the King of Holland. Jerome became the King of a new country he had created called Westphalia. Napoleon had arranged for Joesphine's son, Eugène de Beauharnais, to marry a Bavarian princess and made him Viceroy of Italy. Napoleon himself took the crown of Italy as well as being Emperor of France. The Bonapartes sagged under the weight of their crowns and titles. Madame Mère could hardly have been happier. "Just so long as it lasts," Napoleon could hear her saying in his ear, "just so long as it lasts."

Napoleon was now living in absolute splendour. He and Josephine travelled in the finest carriages, dined off the best china, wore the richest silks and fabrics. New bridges built by Napoleon crossed the Seine and magnificent new quays serviced the boats. New roads cut through the city. Paris was emerging like a butterfly from the darkness of war and revolution. Napoleon was thoroughly enjoying all the luxury. No longer was he the modest, determined general in the scruffy uniform. He was the pampered Emperor in the feathered cap. He had visions of even greater victories, of seizing even more land, of extending his empire even further. He wanted to outstrip his heroes of old, Caesar, Alexander the Great and Charlemagne. He wanted, simply, to rule the world.

Napoleon also found it harder and harder to accept criticism. He hated being contradicted by anyone whether it was his family, the press or his generals and advisors. He didn't really notice that all of his ideas, good or bad, were enthusiastically endorsed. He didn't realise that even his friends were too scared to make him angry. Napoleon, in other words, had changed.

There were other shadows building, shadows that were rapidly joining together to form one big stormy cloud. Though the people of France were so enjoying this, the day of his return, Napoleon knew there was great unhappiness. The people had grown tired of war. So many thousands had died in Napoleon's battles and many, many more had been maimed or injured. While the Emperor's court was rich and well supplied, it was hard for ordinary people to get basic things. The English blockade of French ports had been strengthened after the battle of Trafalgar. This meant no rum, no coffee, no sugar and even no chocolate. Even rich Parisians were forced to suspend a piece of sugar on a string from the ceiling to share for their tea. Each member of the family was allowed to dip the sugar in their cup only briefly.

Napoleon also knew the state treasury was again running low and the stock market was doing poorly. There simply wasn't much money around. This meant many of Napoleon's grand building plans were either going very slowly or had stopped altogether. The Arc de Triomphe looked beautiful but Napoleon didn't know when it would be completed.

Back in the Tuileries Palace where he now lived,

Napoleon tried to get on with the normal duties of an emperor. But there were so many distractions. Every time he dealt with one problem, there seemed to be a dozen more. Take Spain, for instance. Once, Spain had been a friend of France's. Now it was a bitter enemy. Napoleon wanted Spain to be part of his empire and sent an army to conquer it. He thought it would be easy. How wrong he was. The Spaniards weren't fighting fairly, Napoleon thought to himself. They never faced up to his armies. They hid in the hills and forests. They shot at his columns, captured his supplies, killed his messengers. These so-called guerrillas, as they called themselves, weren't brave enough to fight a real battle.

Napoleon felt true anger well up inside him when he thought of the battle of Bailen. What a horrible, mess-up that had been. The French army in Spain was so busy trying to carry away loot and treasure that it hadn't noticed the Spaniards and the English troops nearby. An entire French army had surrendered with hardly a shot being fired in anger. What a disgrace!

Losing battles like that, even though he wasn't there himself, was bad news. It made people think Napoleon was getting weaker, that he could be beaten. The only way to stop such talk was to round up his army once more and win some more battles. If he could just keep going, keep winning, keep making France bigger, keep capturing jewels and money, then no one could ever stop the

Bonapartes, Napoleon thought to himself. Only if he stopped would his empire crumble. He had won glorious battles, even since Austerlitz. At Jena, for instance, in 1806, as well as at Eylau and at Friedland the following year. He couldn't stop now. He decided to lead his army on another excursion. Poland was as good a place as any. It would be useful to build a friendly buffer between himself and Russia. Of course, winter was approaching and that would make fighting in Poland difficult. But Napoleon decided to go for it anyway.

Then Napoleon had a rather awkward decision to make about his wife, the Empress. Napoleon called Josephine to meet him in a reception room in the Tuileries Palace.

"Josephine, my love, my Empress," he said. "You know as well as I that I need an heir. Without one, all of this is lost. All we have done with France, with Europe, will come to nothing. I must have an heir to carry my work forward".

"What about Eugène?" asked Josephine. "You love him like a son, why not make him your heir?"

"I do love Eugène, that is true. But I need an heir from my own body. I need another Napoleon."

"So what would you have me do?" asked Josephine.

"My dear Josephine, we must be divorced and I must take a new wife. I am sorry, but I have no choice."

With that Josephine wailed with grief, then collapsed.

She had to be carried to her chambers.

Napoleon felt terrible but he believed he had no choice. He needed an heir. Without one, he thought his empire was doomed. All his conquests would be nothing more than a short affair soon forgotten by history. Napoleon believed his deeds should always be remembered. Had he not built an empire to rival the greatest the world had known? He now needed a son to carry on his ideas, his vision, his empire.

Napoleon decided that Josephine certainly wouldn't be sent away empty-handed. She would retain the rank of Empress-Queen, three castles, her vast and expensive wardrobe (including 280 pairs of shoes) and several million francs worth of paintings, jewels, gold and silver plate, tapestries, elegant carriages and horses. Napoleon would also pay off her debts (again) and give her an allowance of two million francs a year. This was a more than modest income, by anyone's standards.

Then Napoleon faced the difficult issue of choosing a new wife. Love had nothing to do with it. This was politics. The only two important issues were: would the new wife bear children and was she wealthy and well-connected? There were two leading contenders. The first was Grand Duchess Anna, the 15-year-old sister of the Russian Tsar Alexander. The second possibility was Archduchess Marie Louise, the 18-year-old daughter of the Austrian Emperor Francis. Napoleon knew his new wife would be chosen for him by a special council of state. Madame Mère would have her say this time. So too would the other members of the Bonaparte clan. This was an important family decision and it would be made together.

One day, the special council of state sat to decide which bride they would choose for Napoleon. The council was told the Russian Tsar, Alexander, was not very keen. Ever since Napoleon had shot the Duke of Enghien and beaten the Tsar at Austerlitz, the Tsar had been cold toward the French Emperor. So the council chose the next best thing. Marie Louise of Austria.

The new empress was no beauty, by any means. She had protruding eyes, an ugly big mouth and a square chin. But her own mother had given birth to 13 children so she obviously came from good child-bearing stock. She could be expected to have many children of her own. This was exactly what Napoleon needed. But he didn't have the time to dash halfway across Europe to get married. He had wars to fight. So he sent a special envoy, Marshal Berthier, to do it for him. Berthier's first task was to persuade Marie Louise and her father, the Emperor of Austria, to accept the proposal. So, armed with a miniature portrait of Napoleon set in diamonds and several million francs worth of jewellery, Berthier travelled to Vienna to meet the Austrian royal family.

Marie Louise knew Napoleon would soon be proposing marriage to her. The French ambassador in Vienna had already made some discreet enquiries. Napoleon didn't want to be embarrassed by his proposal being turned down. As expected, the Austrian Emperor agreed to the marriage. Shortly after Berthier arrived in Vienna, handed over the jewels and formally asked for Marie Louise's hand, the marriage ceremony took place. Napoleon wasn't even there. Berthier stood in on Napoleon's behalf, as what is called "a proxy", and then returned to Paris. When she was ready and had packed up her things, Marie Louise travelled to Paris too.

As she neared Paris, the weather turned bad. Marie Louise's carriage rumbled through the mud, the rain beating down on the roof. She sat in the carriage and tried to think what Napoleon would be like. She was a little scared but also excited. Her husband was the most powerful man in the world. Emperors and Kings feared him. His lands stretched from one side of Europe to the other. His court was extremely rich. Marie Louise could look forward to a life of pampered luxury. But what would he be like away from the armies and from the business of state? Was he charming? Was he kind? Would he love her? Would she grow to love him? As she pondered these things, there was a great commotion outside.

Horses galloped up in the darkness, through the rain. Her carriage came to a sudden halt. The next moment, the door of her carriage was flung open.

In from the rain climbed a small man in a black hat and coat with straight hair, a large nose and piercing grey eyes. He was wet through, but he had a smile on his face.

"The Empress of France, I take it?" asked Napoleon, taking Marie Louise's hand and kissing it. He sat beside her. "Welcome to Paris. We have much to talk about."

In the days that followed, Napoleon was surprised at how much he came to love Marie Louise. She was a simple, innocent woman who knew so little of the world. Yet they enjoyed each other's company and spent happy days getting to know each other. Soon, as the

Bonaparte family had hoped, Marie Louise was pregnant. And, on the 20th March 1811, she went into labour.

It was a very difficult and long labour. Napoleon paced up and down as he waited anxiously for news. For hour after hour he waited.

Then, there was a knock at his door. It was the doctor.

"I'm afraid, Emperor, it is not going well," the doctor said.

"Will she live?" asked Napoleon.

"Perhaps," replied the doctor. "Though it may come to a choice. You may have to choose whether the mother or the child will be saved."

"Save the mother," Napoleon said instantly.

"Very well, Emperor," said the doctor, and returned to Marie Louise's bedside.

Napoleon now paced even more anxiously than before. After an unbearably long time, there were more footsteps. They were almost running this time and the knock at the door was loud and rapid.

"Congratulations, Emperor, you have a son."

"And the empress?" asked Napoleon.

"She will be fine. She is just tired. Mother and child are well."

On hearing the news, cannon shots sounded across Paris. They signalled that Napoleon Bonaparte at last had an heir. The city celebrated. Marie Louise would never forget Napoleon's choice and loved him all the more for it. Their child was christened in Notre Dame cathedral soon after the birth. He was given the name François Charles Joseph and the title of King of Rome.

But even these important family matters could not get in the way of Napoleon's grander plan. He still wanted to conquer Europe and then the rest of the world.

This time he led his army into Poland, where the fighting took place midwinter in frozen wastelands. The French soldiers weren't used to fighting in such harsh conditions. They didn't like battles fought in the bone-aching cold or slipping on ice or getting stuck in freezing mud. Though they again met with success, many French lives were lost. The army that loved him so much, was beginning to doubt him.

There was much grumbling among his soldiers and officers about whether it was really necessary to fight a war in such horrible conditions and at such a cost. But Napoleon couldn't stop. He was already

in Poland, why not keep going east? Why not march all the way to Moscow and defeat Russia? Then his empire would be even bigger, even stronger, even richer. Such had been the cost of all his warring that France was running out of both men to serve in the Grand Army and horses to pull its guns, cavalry and equipment. But Napoleon was undeterred. He wanted to put an end, once and for all, to the threat of Russia in the east.

As always, the huge Grand Army followed him into battle. For him, they marched over the empty land in the cold rain. For him, they fought battles and endured the tiredness and the hunger.

The wily Russian Tsar copied the tactics of the Spanish. The Russians fought briefly then retreated, fought and then retreated. With each retreat, Napoleon's supply lines got longer and longer; he lost more horses, more men, more equipment.

He beat the Russians at Smolensk but the Russians pulled back once more. As they retreated, the Russian soldiers destroyed crops and food, water supplies and houses. Napoleon's army was getting tired. His horses ran out of forage.

As summer came to an end and autumn set in, Napoleon should perhaps have had second thoughts about his decision to push on all the way to Moscow. But there were by now no critics left in Napoleon's army and the little general was as stubborn as he was determined.

Not far from Moscow, the Russians gave battle again, this time at Borodino.

This was one of the bloodiest battles in history. As many as 50,000 Frenchmen were killed or maimed in the battle, and around 40,000 Russians. Once again, the Russian army fell back. The way was now open to Moscow.

On 15th September, 1812, Napoleon led his conquering Grand Army into Moscow. What a glorious day it was. At last, Napoleon had conquered Russia. Now Europe was his from west to east, from Boulogne to Vladivostok. Nobody could stop him now. Napoleon was a bit disappointed to find that the Russian Tsar Alexander had fled to distant St Petersburg. But he thought he would settle his troops down in Moscow, see out the winter and force the Tsar to sign a peace treaty in the spring.

A terrible surprise awaited Napoleon. Only one day after he had set up his office in the Kremlin, Moscow was set on fire. Quite deliberately, dozens of arsonists set alight building after building. They thought it was the only way to get rid of the French army.

The once beautiful capital burned like an enormous bonfire. Many of the onion-domed churches with their green cupolas and most of the palaces, homes and shops were made of wood. The fire burned for three days.

By the time the flames had been doused, there wasn't much left of Moscow. Almost all the city's residents

had fled. There was no food, no shelter. Moscow was a charred, smouldering skeleton. Napoleon had no choice. He had to turn his army round once more and march the long, long way back home.

CHAPTER 13 – LONG WAY HOME

Napoleon was cold to his bones. He had been walking forever. There was no other way home. The horses were dead. The roads were muddy and covered in ice. All he could remember was the sound of his boots squelching through the mud, for hour after hour, day after day. At least his clothes were warm. He had a thick fur cape wrapped around him and a velvet hat of deep purple on his head. But nothing could stop the cold coming up through his boots.

He felt so sad when he looked around at his men. His Grand Army was broken. Soldiers with frostbitten feet wrapped in rags stumbled on the frozen roads. Most marched without weapons, many hobbled on sticks. One by one they gave up and fell into the snow to die. Those who fell behind or who wandered off looking for warmth or food were killed. The Russians had not taken kindly to the burning of Moscow. They killed every Frenchman they could find, as cruelly and slowly as they could. They hunted them like animals and strung them up over fires to burn. Many, many died from cold, from hunger and from the angry Russians.

Napoleon couldn't get out of his head the sight of the battlefield at Borodino. He now wished that they had taken another road. By the time they marched home, the bodies had still not been buried after the great battle there. Tens of thousands of bodies, French and Russian, lay where they had died. Many had been partly eaten by wolves. The smell of rotting flesh was awful. The sight was terrible. The army had marched past in silence and had hardly said a word since. Then a few days out of Moscow, a big storm had blown in from the east. It had been the first big storm of winter and had turned a slow, painful march into hell. The roads were soon covered in snow and ice. After the snow came the mud, then more snow again. The Grand Army stumbled and fell. Before long, dead soldiers and decomposing horses lay by the side of the road in their hundreds. Gun carriages, wagons and cannons were left behind. The army, stretched out over 50 miles, was in total disarray.

Finally, the retreat from Moscow became a desperate struggle simply to get home alive. For day after day, week after week they marched. As Napoleon looked at the officers with him, he wondered if anything would be left of his Grand Army by the time they got to Paris. The greatest, biggest best-trained army in history was now little more than a rabble of cold, dirty, hungry men. Napoleon also knew this would please his enemies greatly. His army was crushed. The Austrians, the Russians, the Prussians and the English would soon be preparing to come after him.

Napoleon eventually got home to Paris. He went straight home to the Tuileries Palace to spend time with Marie Louis and François. Over the following weeks, he tried to create a new army to replace the one he had left dead or dying of cold in Russia. But there were no horses and the men he ordered to report for duty were young and had no training. Russia, Austria, Prussia and England, as he expected, joined forces once more to fight the "Corsican Ogre". Napoleon knew he would need every ounce of his strength, every trick up his sleeve and all the luck he could get to save his crown and his dream.

By March 1814, Napoleon was on the verge of exhaustion. For weeks he had been on the move. He had fought a dozen battles in miserable weather. But each victory had led merely to another battle. The armies of Prussia, Russia, England and Austria taunted and tussled with what was left of his forces. After each skirmish, the French army's strength was diminished still more. And still they closed in on Paris.

Napoleon loved to read reports of the numbers of his soldiers and where they were deployed. But these days, it made bad reading. He had only 80,000 soldiers left to defend France. His enemies' armies were much, much bigger. He faced 300,000 Prussian and Russian troops assembled along the Rhine. An Austrian army had crossed through neutral Switzerland. In the far south, England's Duke of Wellington had crossed the Pyrenees mountains at Narbonne with 125,000 troops. The odds were simply overwhelming. Anyone else would have given up. Not Napoleon. For him, nothing was impossible. He ran around like a man possessed. He called more men into the army. He organised civilians into partisan groups. He even formed regiments with customs officials.

"The nation is in danger," he kept saying, "the nation is in danger."

He was right. It wasn't long before Austrian and Prussian forces skipped over the Rhine and marched into France. The cities of eastern France surrendered swiftly and by the end of January, enemy armies were little more than a hundred miles from Paris. Still Napoleon thought he would have one last go to save his empire. He left his brother Joseph in charge of Paris, said goodbye to Marie Louise and to François, now three years old, and embarked on what became known as the Campaign of Miracles.

With his back to the wall, driven on by despair and a hatred of defeat, Napoleon fought some of the most brilliant actions of his entire career. As each enemy army overextended itself in the race to Paris, Napoleon fought them and beat them back. He won three victories in a row in six days. But time was running out. On the night of 23rd March, the allies captured some letters that were on their way to Napoleon from the defenders of Paris. The letters said Paris was undefended, frightened and seething with Napoleon's enemies. The allies immediately decided to press on for the capital, forcing Napoleon to head home.

Then, one day, the worst of all moments arrived. Napoleon looked out from the grand windows of the Tuileries Palace. He felt very bitter and very sad. Not for 300 years had foreign armies marched through the streets of Paris. Now, even as he watched, ranks of Russian cossacks with their furry hats and big boots and Prussian cavalry with their green uniforms and bright plumes rode proudly right down the Champs Elysées. They passed within feet of the Arc de Triomphe, his Arc de Triomphe. What a cheek! Now surely, all was lost.

Through all the months of the Russian campaign, Napoleon had kept a small vial tied around his neck. In it was a sachet of poison. It was the strongest, quickest poison his scientists could devise. It contained crushed flowers of the deadly belladonna plant and of the equally dreaded white hellebore. A little opium was added to take away the grievous pain swallowing such a mixture would cause. Napoleon now sat on his bed and took the vial off from around his neck. He emptied it into a glass of Vin de Constance, his favourite sweet white wine brought all the way from South Africa. He had tried to hand his throne to François, but his enemies had said no. Everything was lost. It was time to end it all. Napoleon swirled the poisonous powder in his glass, gulped it down right to the end and lay down to die.

CHAPTER 14 –
THE DEVIL IS UNCHAINED

There was to be no easy exit from this life for Napoleon. After months and months of safekeeping, the poison in the vial around his neck had lost its potency. He was extremely sick after drinking it, but he survived. He waited to hear what would happen to him. During the month of April, 1814, the emperors and allied generals of Europe met to decide his fate. On the 14th they signed the Treaty of Fontainebleau.

"There is good news and bad news, Emperor," said Berthier. In his hand, he held the Treaty.

"Go on, what is to be my fate?" asked Napoleon.

"You are to remain an Emperor," Berthier said.

"Really?" said Napoleon. "They are not going to kill me?"

"No, they have decided not to kill you. You are to remain an Emperor, but only really in name, Emperor. Your empire is to be made much smaller."

"How much smaller?" asked Napoleon.

"Well, that is the bad news. You will be Emperor of Elba".

"Elba? That tiny island off the French coast? Elba?"

"Yes, Emperor. But you will be free to roam the island as you please and the King has agreed to pay you a monthly salary."

"Which King?" asked Napoleon.

"Why King Louis, the XVIII, of France."

"So I am to be exiled to a small island and paid a small salary by the King of France. It is worse even than I thought. I knew I should have stayed in Egypt!"

But Napoleon had no choice. On the journey to Elba, he read the newspaper reports of events with anger. King Louis XVIII had indeed been put on the French throne. The Bourbon monarchy was back. Napoleon read with sadness how the French people were at first filled with joy at the return of the King. But he was pleased to see that this happiness didn't last long. After Napoleon, the conqueror, the French now had a fat, old king. Louis XVIII was immensely overweight and because of his gout was unable to move without support on either side. He was 58 years old but seemed more like 85. He appeared to care as little for the sufferings of ordinary French people as his royal predecessor, Louis XVI (Louis XVII had only been king of France in name for a few years after his father was killed in the Revolution).

Napoleon read with displeasure how the new king was

moving quickly to reduce the size of Napoleon's army. Officers were discharged by the thousand and replaced by Royalists. Some of these same Royalists had just been fighting against Napoleon's French army. The streets of Paris swarmed with discharged, penniless veterans. In the countryside, the peasants were extremely worried their land would be given back to the rich nobles. It seemed there were many unhappy people in France.

All this was beyond Napoleon now. He soon reached the French coast and on 28th April set sail for Elba, together with his personal staff and a regiment of 600 soldiers of his own imperial guard. To add insult to injury, he left France aboard the British ship *HMS Undaunted*. He was 44 years old and he had finally lost it all. But Napoleon was used to small islands. He had been born on one and now he was back on one once more. Elba was tiny: 18 miles long by 12 across. Altogether, it was a small fraction of the massive empire he had ruled. But at least he was still alive.

Boxed up on his island, Napoleon grew extremely restless. He could hardly sit still for a moment. There was so much he still had to do. He couldn't give up yet. He immediately started a programme of building roads and improving the island's facilities. His mother, Madame Mère and his sister Pauline visited him. He kept asking to see his wife Marie Louise and his son François, but they had been swept away to Marie Louise's father's home in

Vienna and he would never see either of them again.

He always enjoyed catching up with the latest events by reading the Paris newspapers. But one day, he was wracked with grief. Josephine had died. His former wife had continued to attract attention even after Napoleon had been sent to his island. The Russian Tsar Alexander had decided to remain on in Paris after the fall of the Corsican Ogre, and had taken a special liking to Josephine. He had visited her every day. Then, one day in May, when she and the Tsar were out driving in a carriage. Josephine had caught a cold and the cold had turned to pneumonia. A few days later she died in the arms of her son Eugène.

Napoleon wept at the news. He had always loved Josephine. Even though they had been forced to go their separate ways and even though they had fought like cat and dog at times, Josephine had always been his soulmate and his friend. Napoleon also heard rumours that he was to be moved from Elba to an even more remote island. When the French King stopped paying his pension, Napoleon was really fed up. He started planning a return. With so many people unhappy in France, perhaps he just needed to arrive with a small army and the French people would take him back?

On 1st March, 1815, Napoleon secretly sailed from Elba and stepped back on to French soil. He had bolstered the soldiers with him who now numbered more than 1,000. They also had two cannon. It was a far cry from his Grand Army, but at least it was a start. His first target was the nearby garrison of Antibes, but his messengers were arrested when they arrived at the camp. So Napoleon turned with his small army and marched to Grenoble. It was a long and difficult march over very hilly terrain, but it avoided the nearby Royalists.

Once at Grenoble, Napoleon faced his first real test. Here, his 1,000 troops lined up against a much larger French battalion defending the town. As the two small armies stood with their guns pointed at each other, Napoleon walked forward. Alone, he walked toward the facing muskets. "Fire," shouted the officer in charge of the Royalist defenders. Not a single shot echoed out.

"Soldiers!" Napoleon barked. "If there is one among you who wishes to kill his emperor, he can do so. Here I am."

"*Vive L'Empereur*!" the soldiers shouted and rushed to join him. They pushed through the gates of Grenoble, then marched toward Lyon. Word spread across Europe. Newspapers screamed the news: "The devil is unchained."

More and more soldiers joined Napoleon's growing army. One of Napoleon's former generals, Marshal Ney, who now commanded a Royalist corps, was sent to capture Napoleon. "I will bring him to you in an iron cage," Ney told King Louis. But on meeting his old friend, Ney changed his mind and joined Napoleon. In Paris, a joker painted a huge, pretend letter from Napoleon to the King. It said: "My good brother – there is no need to send any more troops – I have enough."

As Napoleon's new army marched to Paris, King Louis and his court dropped everything and fled for Belgium. Napoleon marched straight back into his old rooms at the Tuileries Palace. There he found that the Bourbon fleur-de-lys symbols had simply been glued over the Napoleonic bees on the carpets. He was back. Napoleon explained to anyone who would listen that his pension had not been paid and he was running out of funds. He wrote letters to the emperors and kings of Europe asking for peace.

Napoleon knew that to survive he had to move quickly. He had always believed it was better to take a big gamble and lose rather than sit around waiting for something to happen. From his office in the palace, he ordered that all the French arsenals should be raided in search of arms and ammunition. He assembled his army. Once more he felt the heat of battle surging in his veins. He marched around his office, rattling off orders just like the old days.

When things were in place, Napoleon joined his army once more and marched them secretly and quickly southwest toward Brussels. Not far from the Belgium capital, he positioned his troops and waited near a small town called Waterloo. A very famous battle was about to begin.

As usual, Napoleon was outnumbered. This time, there were two enemy soldiers for every one of his men. Although most of the armies that had attacked him in Paris had gone home months ago – the Russians, for instance, were long gone – two armies were still in the field, the English and the Prussians. The English were led by the Duke of Wellington and the Prussians by General Gebhard von Blucher.

As Napoleon had half the number of soldiers, he knew he would once more have to be clever. He would try his old trick of keeping the two enemy armies apart and then fighting them one at a time. But this time it wasn't going to be as easy as before. Though most of his soldiers were old veterans, he had lost almost all of his senior officers. They had joined the new French army formed when Napoleon was sent to Elba.

"Soldiers!" Napoleon told his army. "For every Frenchman with a heart, the moment has come to conquer or perish!"

But there was to be no glory for Napoleon this time. As Napoleon watched, the English army under Wellington fought harder and better than he had expected. And though the battle could have gone either way for quite some time, Wellington's defence eventually gave the Prussians time to break through. Together, the Prussians and English were too strong for Napoleon.

Just after 8pm on the 18th June, Waterloo was won.

Napoleon had fought his last battle. The bodies of 40,000 soldiers lay dead or dying. Napoleon abandoned his defeated army and fled to Paris. He thought of making a run for it and sailing to America. Perhaps he could raise another army? In the end, though, he decided to throw himself at the mercy of the one country he had never managed to defeat: England. On 15th July, Napoleon boarded the English ship, the *HMS Bellerophon*. He hoped he might be granted asylum to live in England. But this was not to be. He had already escaped once. And the emperors and kings of Europe wanted to make sure he would never escape again.

CHAPTER 15 – MIDDLE OF NOWHERE

Atlantic Ocean, October 17, 1815: "Land," shouted the sailor atop the highest mast. "Land, ahoy!" Down below decks, the officers had just been served dinner. Admiral George Cockburn looked over to Napoleon. "Should we?" he asked.

The group of English and French officers left their meal, stood up and made their way to the bridge deck. It had been 71 days since they had set sail from Plymouth. Land would be a welcome sight. Peering through a spyglass, Napoleon made out the faint outline of a jagged mountain top.

"Diana's Peak," said Admiral Cockburn.

The French party stared in horror at their new home. They saw a great, grey wall of basalt rising out of the ocean. Not a tree or a bush could be seen anywhere. Squashed between two great, slate peaks was Jamestown. It was little more than a few pale houses overhung by the dark, volcanic rock. Artillery bristled from the surrounding cliffs. Welcome to St Helena.

The small island, only ten miles long by seven across, could hardly have been more in the middle of nowhere. It was 1,750 miles from the nearest landfall, the coast of South Africa, and 1,800 miles from the South American shore. "I would have done better to have stayed on Elba," Napoleon thought to himself.

Together with a few of his officers and their wives, an historian, a surgeon, and 11 servants, the former Emperor of France moved into his ramshackle new lodgings. Longwood House was some distance from Jamestown, up a steep road and along a barren plain. Here, surrounded by English soldiers and imprisoned by the endless, empty Atlantic Ocean, the little general would see out the rest of his days.

At first, Napoleon busied himself with fixing up the garden at Longwood House. He was often up at 5am in his a dressing-gown and red morocco slippers giving orders for plants to be moved or holes to be dug. This time, instead of a Grand Army of 200,000 men, he directed a handful of servants and four Chinese labourers.

It was a long, long way from the days of the French empire. He still had his books, though only the campaign library of 600 volumes in six mahogany boxes. He still slept in the iron cot with the green taffeta curtain that had travelled with him to virtually every battlefield in Europe. And he still hoped that instead of the English frigates that floated on the distant horizon and the English soldiers who watched him day and night, one day French ships and French soldiers would appear to fetch him to finish the job he had started.

But it was never to be. Trapped on an island thousands of miles from civilization, the great Napoleon was left with nothing but his memories. In 60 battles and 20 years of power and fame, he had created an empire to rival Ancient Rome. Yet now he had only a well-ordered garden to show for his efforts. "What a story my life has been," he said to himself.

Some say that to make sure he was never seen again, the little general was murdered. They say he was poisoned with arsenic, little by little, year by year until he was dead. Others argue that he gave in to the very illness, stomach cancer, that killed his father.

What is known for sure is that on the night of 4th May 1821, a terrible storm blew in from the south Atlantic. The rain thrashed down, as it had so often on important nights in Napoleon's life. The wind howled. Even the willow tree that Napoleon loved and under which he used to sit gave way. In the aftermath of the storm the next day, Napoleon fought his last fight. At 5.49 that evening, as the cannon sounded to mark the vanishing of the sun below the distant horizon, he died.

He had dreamed one day of ruling the world. He certainly changed it. But when he died, Europe sighed in relief. The little general was gone at last.

KEY DATES

1769	Napoleon born in Corsica
1786	Napoleon becomes a lieutenant in the French army
1789	French Revolution begins
1792	Fall of the French Monarchy
1793	Napoleon commands artillery at siege of Toulon
1795	Napoleon defends Republican government
1796	Napoleon marries Josephine
1796-7	First Italian Campaign
1798-99	Egyptian Campaign
1799	Brumaire coup
1800	Battle of Marengo
1802	Peace of Amiens
1803-5	Plans to invade England
1804	Duke of Enghien executed; Napoleon crowned Emperor
1805	Battles of Ulm and Austerlitz
1806	Battle of Jena
1807	Battles of Eylau and Friedland; Peace of Tilsit
1808-14	Peninsular War
1809	Battle of Wagram
1810	Napoleon marries Marie-Louise of Austria
1812	Napoleon invades Russia
1814	Napoleon abdicates; sent to Elba
1815	Napoleon returns; Battle of Waterloo
1821	Napoleon dies on St Helena

A NOTE ON SOURCES

There have been an estimated 300,000 books written about the life, family and times of Napoleon Bonaparte. This probably makes him the most written about person in history. On average, one book has been published about Napoleon every day since his death in 1821. The amazing thing is few authors agree on even the important events. They can't decide whether he was a great general or even how he died. For every author who says one thing, you will find another three saying something different.

I have based this book on three key elements: on hundreds of letters and documents written by Napoleon himself, on two important biographies of Napoleon, one by J Holland Rose and one by Robert Asprey and finally on a range of dozens of interesting books about different elements of the life of Napoleon. Among these were Alistair Horne's *How Far from Austerlitz?* B Ratcliffe's *Prelude to Fame*, Christopher Hibbert's *Napoleon: His wives and women*, and the *Murder of Napoleon* by Ben Weider and David Hapgood.

I also found the website, http://www.historyguide.org very useful.

QUIZ

After you've finished the book, test yourself and see how well you remember what you read.

1. What was Napoleon's favourite sweet?
   Lemon sherbets
   Liquorice
   Wine gums

2. How many children did Napoleon's parents have?
   4
   8
   24

3. Who did Napoleon's parents ask to pay their son's fees at Brienne military school?
   Their next-door neighbour
   His older brother
   The King of France

4. What did students of the Ecole Militaire in Paris receive when they graduated?
   A sword
   A pat on the head
   A gun

5. When the French Revolution started in 1789, Napoleon supported it because:
   He wanted to be king
   He thought ordinary people should be in charge of the government
   He liked the weird new calendar

6. Napoleon joined the army as a soldier in the:
   Artillery
   Tank regiment
   Catering corps

7. Which countries fought with the Royalists at the Battle of Toulon in 1793?
   England and Australia
   England and Spain
   England and Russia

8. Why did Napoleon refuse to join the Army of the West?
   Because he wanted to fight abroad
   Because he didn't want to leave his mother
   Because he didn't get on with the general

9. Who led the Royalist uprising that Napoleon defeated in Paris in 1795:
   General Danican
   Lieutenant Parmesan
   Captain Cannon

10. How did Josephine's first husband die?
   He was shot in battle
   She poisoned him
   He was beheaded by guillotine

11. Napoleon won the battle of Montenotte in 1796 by:
   Tricking the Sardinian army into leaving Genoa
   Pretending he was going to surrender
   Offering a free lunch to all the Sardinian soldiers

12. Why did Napoleon want to conquer Egypt?
   To recruit more soldiers for his army
   To get control of a route to India
   Because he wanted to be mummified after his death

13. In what formation did the French army go into the Battle of the Pyramids?
   Squares
   Triangles
   Columns

14. The scientific institute that Napoleon established in Egypt investigated ways to:
   Turn water into wine
   Purify water from the Nile
   Find water in the desert

15. When Napoleon returned home after being defeated in Egypt, the people of France:
   Cheered him as a great hero
   Made fun of him as a sad loser

Didn't realise he was back because he was dressed as an old woman

16. The French fleet commanded by Admiral Villeneuve was defeated at:
   The Battle of the Bulge
   The Battle of Trafalgar
   The Battle of Austerlitz

17. Napoleon gave his longed-for son the title of:
   The Duke of Paris
   The King of Rome
   The Prince of Bel Air

18. For Napoleon, the Battle of Borodino was:
   A costly victory
   A humiliating defeat
   A close shave

19. Napoleon's last battle took place at:
   Trafalgar
   Waterloo
   Paddington

20. Where was Napoleon sent after abdicating as emperor in 1814?
   The island of Elba
   The Falkland Islands
   The Isle of Wight

Dear Reader,

No matter how old you are, good books always leave you wanting to know more. If you have any questions you would like to ask the author, **Adrian Hadland**, about **Napoleon** please write to us at: SHORT BOOKS, 15 Highbury Terrace, London N5 1UP.

If you enjoyed this title, then you would probably enjoy others in the series. Why not click on our website for more information and see what the teachers are being told? **www.theshortbookco.com**

All the books in the WHO WAS... series are available from TBS, Distribution Centre, Colchester Road, Frating Green, Colchester, Essex CO7 7DW
(Tel: 01206 255800), at £4.99 + P&P.